The

POWER

of a

HUMBLE LIFE

ALSO BY RICHARD E. SIMMONS III

REFLECTIONS ON THE EXISTENCE OF GOD
A Series of Essays

THE REASON FOR LIFE
Why Did God Put Me Here?

WISDOM
Life's Great Treasure

SEX AT FIRST SIGHT
Understanding the Modern Hookup Culture

A LIFE OF EXCELLENCE
Wisdom for Effective Living

THE TRUE MEASURE OF A MAN
How Perceptions of Success, Achievement & Recognition
Fail Men in Difficult Times

RELIABLE TRUTH
The Validity of the Bible in an Age of Skepticism

REMEMBERING THE FORGOTTEN GOD
The Search for Truth in the Modern World

SAFE PASSAGE
Thinking Clearly about Life & Death

The
POWER
of a

HUMBLE LIFE

QUIET STRENGTH
IN AN AGE OF ARROGANCE

RICHARD E. SIMMONS III

UNION HILL
PUBLISHING

Union Hill Publishing

The Power of a Humble Life
Quiet Strength in an Age of Arrogance

Union Hill Publishing
200 Union Hill Drive, Suite 200
Birmingham, AL 35209

www.richardesimmons3.com

ISBN 978-1-939358-15-8

3   4   5   6   7   8   9   10

Printed in the United States of America

To my wonderful wife Holly,
my soulmate and very best friend.

CONTENTS

INTRODUCTION

Back in 2009 I wrote the book *The True Measure of a Man*, which was based on a series of talks I had given to a large group of businessmen. These talks focused on how hard it generally was to face the financial challenges in our lives in light of the economic hardship that the entire world was then experiencing. Those were unprecedented times, and there was a great deal of uncertainty everywhere. Almost every man I knew was wondering what was going to happen next and how it would impact him and his family. What made it so difficult was that much of what was taking place in the economy was completely out of their control.

Here we are, almost nine years later, and everything has changed. The economy is good, the unemployment rate is low, and the Dow Industrial Average is at an all-time high. The fear has subsided, and for most people, life is good.

The book you are about to read, *The Power of a Humble Life*, is in many ways a sequel to *The True Measure of a Man*, although it is not targeting just men. This is a book for men, women, young and old, and the message has the potential to be life-changing.

I dig into an issue, which plagues us all, though most of us are completely unaware that it exists in our lives, and I share what I consider to be life's greatest paradox. Many of God's important truths are foreign to the world we live in because they are so counterintuitive. For this reason, biblical truth often comes across as utter foolishness to some people.

What we do not recognize is that very often the wisdom of God, the truth of God, is paradoxical. Paradox is defined in *Webster's* as "a tenet that is contrary to received opinion. A statement or principle that is seemingly contradictory and opposed to common sense, but may in fact be true."

In this book, the paradox that I discuss is essential to a life well-lived. It strikes right at the heart of who we are as human beings, and its ramifications are incredibly significant in all areas of our lives. It is of foundational importance if we want to live an exceptional life.

Life's greatest paradox is found in the title of the book—our strength is found in humility. This interesting and challenging concept, certainly not taught at Harvard Business School, is clearly counterintuitive.

As we explore the underpinnings of this great paradox, we will begin with the thorny issue of pride and arrogance and continue on by exploring the power of humility. At the end, I believe that you will clearly see the power of a humble life.

~ I ~

OUR GREATEST DILEMMA

PRIDE HAS BEEN THE CHIEF CAUSE OF
MISERY IN EVERY NATION AND EVERY
FAMILY SINCE THE WORLD BEGAN.

– *C. S. Lewis*

~ I ~

OUR GREATEST
DILEMMA

I think at times it is very difficult for us to understand the human condition and the thoughts that go through our hearts and our minds. For instance, why do we feel so compelled to impress other people? What is that all about? And why are we always comparing ourselves with others? Why can't we just be content with who we are and what we have? Then there is, of course, the big question. It is the one question we are always asking ourselves. It often seems to be the central question that must finally be answered before we will make certain decisions or take definitive courses of action. It is a question that I believe haunts many people's lives:

What will people think about me?

This question operates in our lives in some form or fashion and can impact us emotionally, psychologically, and even spiritually. I am sure you recognize this to be true of your life, but what is this really all about? There is a simple answer: the pride of life.

C.S. Lewis is considered by many to be one of the greatest authors ever. More than 300 million copies of his books have been sold; and though he died in 1963, hundreds of thousands of his books are still purchased each year. One of his most well-known works is *Mere Christianity*, in which he intellectually lays out a defense of the Christian faith. In a section labeled "Christian Behavior," he discusses topics such as cardinal virtues, social and sexual morality, forgiveness, charity, and hope, followed by a chapter entitled, "The Great Sin." Lewis opens this chapter with the following words:

> There is one vice of which no man in the world is free, and which everyone in the world loathes when he sees it in someone else, and of which hardly any people, except maybe some Christians, ever imagine that they are guilty themselves. I have heard people admit that they are bad-tempered, or that they cannot keep their heads about girls, or drink, or even that they are cowards, but I don't think that I have ever heard anyone accuse himself of this vice. And, at the same time, I have very seldom met anyone, again, other than some Christians, who showed the slightest mercy to it in others. There is no fault which makes a man more unpopular, and no fault of which we are more unconscious of than others, and the more we have it ourselves, the more we dislike it in others. The vice I'm talking of is pride, or self-conceit.

People struggle with pride more than anything else. This sin is deadly because it is so insidious. Lewis describes pride as a spiritual cancer that destroys our ability to genuinely love others and prevents us from being content. As a spiritual cancer, pride slowly grows and develops in our lives, becoming well-established without our knowledge. Lewis says that pride is purely spiritual; it originates straight from hell and consequently is far more subtle and deadly than all other sins. We readily recognize it and hate it in others, but most of us believe that we are in no way afflicted by it.

We often misunderstand the word "pride." Webster's defines it in two ways: The first is a "justifiable self-respect"—the idea of taking pride in doing the best that you can do. The second definition is what Lewis is speaking of—"an arrogance, an unreasonable conceit

---

PRIDE GETS NO PLEASURE OUT OF HAVING
SOMETHING, ONLY OUT OF HAVING MORE THAN THE
NEXT MAN. (C.S. LEWIS)

and feeling of superiority." The Greeks called it hubris, which means to have too high a view of oneself.

THE NATURE OF PRIDE

To get to the heart of this issue, we need to understand where pride originates. There is an interesting verse in the book of Ecclesiastes that provides some great insight.

> I have seen that every labor and every skill which is done is the result of rivalry between a man and his neighbor . . . (Ecclesiastes 4:4).

Most of us are rarely satisfied and content in our own work and achievements. We constantly compare ourselves with other people and desire to be more successful than they are because we have a great desire to impress others. Despite our many achievements, we don't feel we are successful unless other people are aware of them. In other words, we seek more than just success—we long for proper recognition of our achievements.

Why are we always comparing ourselves with others? Why do we hide our weaknesses and failures? Why are we constantly wondering if our lives measure up to others in our sphere of influence?

Again, from Mere Christianity, C.S. Lewis puts it this way:

> Now, what you want to get clear is this, that pride is essentially competitive. It's competitive by its very nature. While the other vices are competitive only, so to speak, by accident, pride gets no pleasure out of having something, only out of having more of it than the next man. We say that people are proud of being rich, or clever, or good-looking, but they are not. They are proud of being richer, or cleverer, or better-looking than others. If everyone else became equally rich, or clever, or good-looking, there would be nothing to be proud about. It's the comparison that makes you proud. The pleasure of being above the rest.

Lewis is saying that we pride ourselves on being wealthier, better-look-ing, more successful, or more intelligent than those around us. How-ever, when we find ourselves in the presence of those who are better in those areas than we are, we feel deflated. We lose all the pleasure we had when we felt superior. In reality, the pleasure stems from our arrogance. We have an exaggerated sense of our own importance or abilities and take pleasure in having more than the next person.

In his book, *Searching for God Knows What*, Donald Miller shares some great insight into the issue of pride. Using his imagination, he began to wonder, if an alien from another planet came to observe our lives here on earth, how he would describe us to his superiors once he returned to his planet. Miller reflected on this a great deal. Late one night, he woke up, got out of bed, and penned the following thoughts from an alien's point of view:

> Humans, as a species, are constantly, and in every way, comparing themselves to one another, which, given the brief nature of their existence, seems an oddity and, for that matter, a waste. Never-theless, this is the driving influence behind every human's social development, their emotional health and sense of joy, and, sadly, their greatest tragedies. It is as though something that helped them function and live well has gone missing, and they are pining for that missing thing in all sorts of odd methods, none of which are working. The greater tragedy is that very few people under-stand they have the disease. This seems strange as well because it is obvious. To be sure, it is killing them, and yet sustaining their social and economic systems. They are an entirely beautiful peo-ple with a terrible problem.

Miller says the alien would not understand our lives, particularly what we watch on television, because the plots on these shows are about desperately trying to find all the things missing from our souls. If the alien had the opportunity to speak to us, he would ask, "Why are you so obsessed?"

> You have to wear a certain kind of clothes, drive a certain car, speak a certain way, live in a certain neighborhood, whatever, all

of it so you can be higher on an invisible hierarchy. It's an obsession! You are trying to feel right by comparing yourself to others. It is ridiculous. Who told you there was anything wrong with you in the first place?

Without realizing it, the alien sees what pride does to our lives.

OUR NEED FOR GLORY

In his Pulitzer Prize winning book, *The Denial of Death*, Ernest Becker writes about our great need for what he calls "cosmic significance." He says this need is so powerful that whatever we end up basing our identity on becomes our deity. This need for cosmic significance explains so much of our natural tendency to be full of pride.

Dr. Tim Keller provides profound insight into this need we have for significance and how we allow it to corrupt our lives. Keller addresses this in a commentary on Philippians 2:3, which says,

> Do nothing from selfish ambition or vain conceit . . . The phrase "selfish ambition" actually means "vainglory." It comes from the Greek word *kenodoxia*. The word *doxa* means "glory." The word kenodoxia means a person is empty or starving for glory. Paul warns against selfish ambition, while acknowledging we are naturally hungry for glory.

In the Bible, the word "glory" means importance. It means "to matter." Fundamentally we are haunted by a deep fear that our lives don't really matter. Keller says the worst thing for a human being is really not being disliked or vilified but instead being ignored and considered insignificant. The human heart fears being so unimportant and worthless in the eyes of others that our lives don't matter to the people around us. For this reason, though we may not be aware of it, every human heart in its deepest recesses is seeking extensive glory.

We are driven to win the approval of others because we are starved for glory. A real and fundamental instability resides in our hearts because it is so easy to feel small and insignificant. As a result, we constantly look for ways to convince the world and ourselves that we matter and that our lives are important.

Vanity Fair magazine featured an interesting interview with pop icon Madonna in which you can see this desire for cosmic significance. Madonna commented:

> I have an iron will, and all of my will has always been to conquer some horrible feeling of inadequacy . . . I push past one spell of it and discover myself as a special human being and then I get to another stage and think I'm mediocre and uninteresting. . . Again and again. My drive in life is from this horrible fear of being mediocre. And that's always pushing me, pushing me. Because even though I've become Somebody, I still have to prove that I'm *Somebody*. My struggle has never ended and it probably never will.

From this interview, you can see Madonna's fear of being mediocre and of losing her status as a music icon. The ultimate fear of all human beings is to be a nobody and not matter to anyone.

So how do we handle this dilemma? We take matters into our own hands and seek to glorify ourselves. We travel through life on an unending quest to prove to the world our lives matter and that we are important. What better way to do that than to prove we are better or superior to those around us? This striving lies at the heart of pride and arrogance. However, even if we do find the success and fame that make us feel significant, we still have to deal with the reality that these will eventually fade. They will not last because we are disintegrating. We yearn for a glory that is permanent, but our lives are slowly passing away.

We will never find peace and contentment in this life until we come to terms with this conundrum. The ultimate solution is humility. The humble are continually at peace with who they are in the eyes of others. They are content with their position in life and what they possess. The humble are the only ones who are delivered from this great drive to prove to the world that "I am important!"

THE DEVASTATION
OF PRIDE

WE MUST PREPARE FOR PRIDE AND
KILL IT EARLY—OR IT WILL KILL
WHAT WE ASPIRE TO.

– *Ryan Holiday, author*

~ 2 ~

THE DEVASTATION
OF PRIDE

The great French author Victor Hugo remarked, "Pride is the fortress of evil in a man." G.K. Chesterton said, "Pride is a poison so very poisonous that it not only poisons the virtues, it even poisons the other vices."

Pride is often the sin that lies beneath so many of our flaws. I remember hearing Charlie Munger of Berkshire Hathaway remark about the corruption on Wall Street that contributed to the financial crisis back in 2008. He said most people blamed it all on greed. However, Munger believes so many of the traders were driven to unethical behavior when they learned a colleague several doors down was making a million dollars a year more than they were. They were controlled by pride and jealousy, not greed.

Bloomberg television, a very popular business channel, has a regular program called *Game Changers*. The show features the life stories of influential leaders who have had an impact on the world of business. One of their most interesting programs covered the life of Larry Ellison, the CEO and founder of Oracle Corporation, an incredibly successful computer software company. Ellison is currently the fifth highest person on the *Forbes 400 Richest Americans* list. His current net worth is 49 billion dollars.

You would think Larry Ellison has it made with nothing to worry about. However, his life is fixated on Bill Gates, the founder of Microsoft. Ellison compares his life, his company, and particularly his wealth to that of Gates and Microsoft. Those who have worked for him will tell you that his greatest desire in life is to dethrone Gates and be recognized as America's richest person. You would think he could find contentment with all of his wealth and accomplishments, but he continually compares himself to Gates and is driven to overtake him. There was an article in Harvard Business Review that blamed it on Ellison's greed. However, this discontentment is clearly what pride does to a person. As C.S. Lewis put it: "It is the comparison that makes you proud: the pleasure of being above the rest."

> "PRIDE IS A POISON, SO VERY POISONOUS, IT NOT ONLY POISONS THE VIRTUES, IT EVEN POISONS THE OTHER VICES." (G. K. CHESTERSON)

What I find to be so fascinating are the strong words that people use to describe pride. C.S. Lewis concludes that it is the "essential vice, the utmost evil, the complete anti-God state of mind." And yet so many of us are not even aware of its presence in our lives and the potential harm that always accompanies it.

Our lives are so deeply influenced by pride. Though its impact on us is pervasive, let's examine how pride impacts our character, our peace of mind, our effectiveness in our work, and then consider its dark destructive nature.

THE EROSION OF CHARACTER

Albert Einstein believed that the French philosopher and mathematician Blaise Pascal was one of the greatest intellects to ever live. Pascal had great insight into the human heart and understood the battles we have with pride. In his great work *Pensées* he says,

> It's the nature of self-esteem and of the human self to love only one's self and to consider one's self alone. But what can a man do?

He wants to be great but he finds that he is small. He wants to be happy and finds that he is unhappy. He wants to be perfect and finds that he is riddled with imperfections. He wants to be the object of men's affection and esteem and sees that his faults deserve only their dislike and contempt. The embarrassing position in which he finds himself produces in him the most unjust and criminal passion that can possibly be imagined. He conceives a mortal hatred of the truth which brings him down to earth and convinces him of his faults. He would like to be able to annihilate it, and not being able to destroy it in himself, he destroys it in the minds of other people. That is to say, he concentrates all his efforts on concealing his faults, both from others, and from himself, and cannot stand being made to see them, or their being seen by other people.

Consider what Pascal is saying. We have this great desire to win man's approval and admiration. Therefore we seek to create a picture we want the world to see that impresses those around us. This picture creates the appearance that *my* life is prosperous, *my* relationships are flourishing, and *I* am a highly competent person who has his act together. However, we all know the truth about ourselves. Pascal says that, over time, our lives are riddled with imperfections in that we all have weaknesses, inadequacies, and many types of fears. So what is a person to do? We hide our true selves from the outside world. We fake it. We hide behind smiling, pretty faces that we put on to impress the public.

However, in hiding our true selves, we fail to realize that we become imposters. Life becomes one great pretense, and we do not realize we are guilty of duplicity. Webster's says that duplicity is "a contradictory doubleness of thought, speech or action. It is hiding one's true intentions by deceptive words or actions."

A person who is guilty of duplicity ultimately has little or no integrity. Integrity means to have a unified soul where our thoughts, our words, and our actions are aligned with each other. Therefore, if the pride in our life leads us to be consistently duplicitous in our nature and in our dealings with others, you can see how it will erode our character.

If we cannot be transparent with ourselves and with others, then who are we? Tim Keller says, "All of us, without God's help, live lives of illusion. We spend almost all of our lives trying to prove to other people and ourselves that we are something other than what we really are."

In his wonderful book, *Disarming the Secular Gods*, Dr. Peter Moore says that arrogant people are narcissists, and they see the world as a mirror. He says,

> Coming into a room full of people, they don't see other people with needs, problems, and life experiences to learn from. What they see is an audience, people to impress, to be admired by, and from whom to gain a measure of self-esteem. Because of their underlying insecurity, they will tend to gravitate to those who radiate celebrity, charisma, power, and influence. These are the people who must be impressed and charmed, and by whom it is essential to be admired. If personal values must be bent in the process, so be it. They are totally subservient to this need. It will be expected that relationships will become manipulative and will be short-lived, because self-absorption prevents them from being truly faithful despite an intent hunger for something lasting and deep.

Dr. Moore is revealing that pride has so impacted us that outward appearance is much more important than inward character. Image rules over substance.

Stephen Covey captured our dilemma when he said, "The effort to put on a front puts one on a treadmill that seems to go faster, almost like chasing a shadow." For so many people it proves to be their undoing. When image and appearance become preeminent in our lives, the heart, the soul, and the character suffer from negligence.

THERE IS NO PEACE FOR THE PROUD

The proud person has a very difficult time finding peace in his life, for he is always worrying what people think about him. Journalist

David Brooks of the *New York Times* believes the proud are unstable because they attempt to establish their self-worth by winning the approval of others, making them utterly dependent on the gossipy,

---

WHEN IMAGE AND APPEARANCE BECOME PREEMINENT
IN OUR LIVES, THE HEART, THE SOUL, AND THE
CHARACTER SUFFER FROM NEGLIGENCE.

---

unstable crowd surrounding them. For this reason, the proud person becomes insecure and is robbed of a peaceful heart.

For most of us, life is all about "what I do." This generally is one of the first questions we ask of a new acquaintance. However, life is not only about "what I do" but also about "how successful I am at what I do." Then we naturally bring others into the equation and begin to wonder, "What do you think about what I do? How do you rate what I do?" It is then only a matter of time before we ask the question, "What if I fail at what I do? What would you think of me then? Would you value me or would you think I'm a loser?"

Fear of failure is one of our greatest fears. It is a psychological death. Bernie Madoff, perpetrator of the largest financial fraud in U.S. history, in his first interview from prison said he was motivated to pull off his grand Ponzi scheme because he feared failure. As he put it, "I did not want to lose the honor and esteem of men." David Sokol was considered by many to be the person who would one day replace Warren Buffett as the CEO of Berkshire Hathaway before he was forced to resign because of unethical conduct. Sokol was able to ascend the corporate ladder because of his unbelievable work ethic, largely stemming from his fear of failing. A very wealthy business-man confided in me that every day when his feet hit the floor, he is motivated by one thing: fear of failure. It seems that most of us are not driven to succeed, we are driven not to fail. We are not running *towards* something positive; rather we are sprinting *away* from failure.

If we want to change, there are two important questions we

should all ask ourselves. How different would my life be if I did not fear failure? And what would my life be like if I did not worry about what people think about me? Not being smothered by worry would change everything because our fear would diminish and we would be able to enjoy peace.

PRIDE AND EFFECTIVE WORK

Pride and arrogance manifest themselves most frequently in the workplace. Our work is clearly visible and easily measurable; for many of us, it is the part of life that lets us know if we are successful. A great deal of comparison goes on in the workplace accompanied by a high fear of failure. At the end of the day, the size of the paycheck reveals a great deal about ability and performance—at least, that is the way most people measure their lives.

What many people do not recognize is how pride impairs our ability to learn, grow, and thrive in our careers, particularly if we are in a leadership role. Arrogant people naturally assume that they know all that is important to know and therefore see no need to learn new things and have no interest in receiving constructive criticism. Author John Dickson says he sees this happen, particularly at conferences he attends.

> Every conference seems to have a Proud Peter. He's the guy in your organization who is moderately talented and charming but whose years in the business have created an inflexibility when it comes to learning from others or implementing changes. His natural wit is able to point out the smallest difficulty with a new idea, and so he quickly convinces himself and sometimes others that the old way—his way—is probably best.
>
> Perhaps it's just my imagination, but I think I can often spot the Proud Peters when I address various audiences. He typically sits in the back with arms folded or behind his head, and throughout the talk he quips to his buddies, who politely smile. He never takes notes—that would be too keen—but he is frequently the

first to raise a hand during the Q&A. He might damn the speaker with faint praise or else pose a question designed to sound clever. Afterward in the staff debriefing, I imagine he resists adopting any fresh insights. He is closed to new thoughts (that aren't his own) and rarely submits himself to review or criticism. His pride impedes his progress.

Dr. J.P. Kotter, author and professor at Harvard Business School, has observed: "Arrogant managers can over-evaluate their current performance and competitive position, listen poorly and learn slowly."

The great literary critic G.K. Chesterton was convinced that pride and arrogance were the main causes of human mediocrity, giving us the false belief that we have arrived. As a result, we feel sufficient and think there is really little else to learn.

Pride is particularly destructive to those in high positions of leadership. Several years ago, an article appeared in the *Harvard Business Review* on why leaders in various business organizations fail. The core data came from a study that revealed the following four primary factors that brought about the failures of those senior leaders:

- They were *authoritarian*—controlling, demanding, not listening to others.
- They were *autonomous*—little accountability, aloof, and isolated.
- They committed *adultery*.
- They became more and more *arrogant*.

I believe the underlying reason these leaders encountered failure can be summed up by these words from the study: *feeling and acting as if they were superior to all others.* If you think you are superior to everyone in your organization, you will find yourself believing that you can treat people however you want, sleep with whomever you choose, and spend the organization's money at will. Basically, you believe you have free rein to do whatever you want. Senator John Edwards of Virginia confessed to having an extramarital affair with a woman during his campaign. His explanation was, in essence, that he had arrived at a point where he did not think the rules applied to him.

Eight years after publishing his incredible, best-selling book, *Good to Great*, Stanford professor Jim Collins wrote another insightful book entitled, *How the Mighty Fall*. He and his team of researchers were seeking to understand the decline and fall of once great companies. They came up with a model that consists of five stages that proceed in sequence as the companies diminish in strength. It is not surprising that Stage 1 is arrogance. People come to regard their company's success as an entitlement, and they lose sight of the true underlying factors that led to the company's success in the first place. They do not seek to continually improve their organization but take the attitude, "We will continue to keep things just the way they are and will continue to be successful because we are such a great company."

Collins shares a great true story of how this can happen:

In the late 1950s, a small, unknown company had a very big idea: "to bring discount retailing to rural and small town areas." It became one of the first companies to bet its future on this concept, and it built a substantial early lead by adopting everyday low prices for everything, not just specific lure-the-consumer items. Its visionary leader created an ethos of partnership with his people, engineered sophisticated information systems, and cultivated a performance-driven culture, with store managers reviewing weekly scorecards at 5 a.m. every Monday morning. Not only did the company decimate Main Street stores in small towns, but it also learned how to beat its primary competitor, Kmart, in head-to-head competition. Every dollar invested in its stock at the start of 1970 and held through 1985 grew more than six thousand percent.

So, now, what is the company?

If you answered Wal-Mart, good guess. But wrong.

The answer is Ames Department Stores.

Ames began in 1958 with the same idea that eventually made Wal-Mart famous and did so four years before Sam Walton opened his first Wal-Mart store. Over the next two decades, both companies built seemingly unstoppable momentum, Wal-Mart growing in the mid-South and Ames in the Northeast. From 1973 to 1986, Ames's and Wal-Mart's stock performances roughly tracked each other, with both companies generating returns over nine times the market.

So where is Ames at the time of this writing?

Dead. Gone. Never to be heard from again. Wal-Mart is alive and well, #1 on the Fortune 500 with $379 billion in annual revenues.

What happened? What distinguished Wal-Mart from Ames?

A big part of the answer lies in Walton's deep humility and learning orientation. In the late 1980s, a group of Brazilian investors bought a discount retail chain in South America. After purchasing the company, they figured they'd better learn more about discount retailing, so they sent off letters to about ten CEOs of American retailing companies, asking for a meeting to learn about how to run the new company better. All the CEOs either declined or neglected to respond, except one: Sam Walton.

When the Brazilians deplaned at Bentonville, Arkansas, a kindly, white-haired gentleman approached them, inquiring, "Can I help you?"

"Yes, we're looking for Sam Walton."

"That's me," said the man. He led them to his pickup truck, and the Brazilians piled in along Sam's dog, Ol' Roy.

Over the next few days, Walton barraged the Brazilians with question after question about their country, retailing in Latin America, and so on, often while standing at the kitchen sink washing and drying dishes after dinner. Finally, the Brazilians realized, Walton—the founder of what may well become the world's first trillion-dollar-per-year corporation—sought first and foremost to learn from them, not the other way around.

Sam Walton was always worried about Wal-Mart's success. He wanted to instill his sense of purpose and to maintain the humble inquisitiveness that would keep the company on the right path, beyond his own lifetime. Part of his answer to keep the company from becoming arrogant was to hand the company's CEO role over to an equally inquisitive leader, the modest and low-profile David Glass. Most people in the world of business were not familiar with Glass, but he had learned from Walton that Wal-Mart does not exist for the grandeur of its leaders, it exists for their customers. Glass passionately believed in Wal-Mart's core purpose, to help people of average means afford more of the goods previously available only to the wealthy. He was very focused on hiring the best people, building a great culture, and expanding into new arenas, while steadfastly adhering to the principles that made Wal-Mart a great company.

This was quite a contrast to the strategy pursued by Ames. Where Sam Walton engineered a smooth transition to a homegrown employee who understood all of the drivers of Wal-Marts success, Ames brought in an outsider to replace Herb Gilman, their CEO. His replacement, though a very capable leader, moved the company in a different direction as he boldly sought to redefine the company. While Wal-Mart sought to maintain a near fanaticism about its core purpose, values, and culture, Ames did just the opposite, expecting quick growth.

Collins says that arrogant leaders believe that they will continue to be successful no matter what the organization decides to do or not do. It is the humble leader who has a learning predisposition, recognizing there is so much that he and those who lead the company do not know. No matter how successful they become, humble leaders remain students of their work, relentlessly asking questions and always seeking continuous improvement.

THE DARK, DESTRUCTIVE SIDE OF PRIDE

Brian Mahan, a theologian at Emory University, wrote a wonderful book entitled: *Forgetting Ourselves on Purpose: The Vocation and Ethics of Ambition*. Mahan wrote that we do not often realize there is a real dark side to pride, particularly as it relates to how we compare ourselves to others. He puts it this way:

> In American society, individual achievement is supremely important. In itself, this is neither good nor bad. It's merely part

of the script. The trouble is that it becomes difficult to assess achievement and monitor happiness without surrendering to the impulse to adopt comparison as a prime measure of individual worth. Some comparisons are harmless enough, and many are, in any case, unavoidable. We take standardized tests. We get accepted or rejected by various degree programs, we accept a job that someone else does not get, and we lose a promotion that goes instead to a colleague. But there is a darker side to comparison. It's the dirty little secret of our society, and we all share in the effort to keep it under wraps. We all know the dark conversations in our hearts, even if only intermittently and selectively, and most of us choose to keep them to ourselves.

You may remember the story of Mark and Lori Hacking. It did not receive a great deal of publicity because Mark Hacking eventually confessed to killing his wife, Lori, and so there was no high profile trial. The story is heartbreaking. The Hackings seemed to be living a normal life together. Mark Hacking, by all accounts, was fun to be around, a loving husband who desired to become a doctor like his father and older brother. However, in the hours when he was supposedly studying for medical exams, Hacking often was hanging out at a neighborhood store, refilling sodas, eating hot dogs, and smoking Camel Menthols. He convinced his wife to pack up and move to North Carolina so that he could attend medical school, where, it turns out, he wasn't even enrolled. He kept textbooks open and spread around his apartment, but in fact, he had dropped out of college long before.

Finally his deception caught up with him when Lori discovered that he was deceiving them all. He had never graduated from college nor applied to medical school. When she confronted him, instead of owning up to it, he made the decision to kill her. His family, of course, was shocked and devastated by this revelation. His father, Douglas Hacking, a prominent physician said, "Mark had two brothers who are high achievers, he felt pressure to excel as well." Brian Hamilton, one of Mark's best friends, put it this way: "Failure was just not an option for Mark."

Mark Hacking compared himself to his older brothers and believed if he were to be a real man, he would need to be a high achiever
like them. You can clearly see the dark side of pride demonstrated as
this man was trying to live up to a high standard; and when he could
not, he used deception to pretend to be something he was not. As a
result of being found out, he was then willing to kill his wife instead
of being exposed as a fake.

Several years ago, National Geographic had a four-hour special on
9/11 and the events that led up to it, taking viewers back to when the
Soviet Union invaded Afghanistan. The head of the Afghan freedom
fighters, who were fighting against the Soviets, was none other than
Osama bin Laden. What is ironic was the United States was providing
him with all types of supplies and equipment at the time. Eventually
the Soviets abandoned Afghanistan. Then in 1991, Saddam Hussein
invaded Kuwait, which was right on the border of Saudi Arabia. Bin
Laden approached the Saudi royal family and asked them to allow his
men to defend them against the Iraqis. The Royal family turned him
down and instead looked to the United States for protection. Apparently, bin Laden felt humiliated by this refusal. National Geographic
points out that this humiliation was the root that led to his hatred
of Saudi Arabia and the United States. Clearly, a man's pride is a
powerful force in his life, and it makes you wonder how world events
have been shaped over the years by pride and arrogance.

It is also amazing how the pride of parents has such an impact
on how they raise their children, and what they expect from their
children. Sociologist Anthony Campolo wrote in his book, *Seven
Deadly Sins:*

> We will never know how many children have had their lives made
> miserable by being pushed to achievements which makes their
> parents look good. Children who are driven to psychological ex-
> haustion for academic achievement often know that their labor
> is primarily to enhance the status of their parents. Behind the
> claims that the parents expect the children to do well, because
> success in school will increase their options, is the ugly reality

that the achievements of the children visibly demonstrate the superiority of the parents.

Sports are ruined for many teenagers. There is not much fun on most varsity teams because there is a deadly seriousness about the games being played. From Little League through interscholastic sports, the omnipresent parents are pushing their children in order to gratify their own ego needs.

Two years ago there was a very sad but intriguing article in *The Atlantic* magazine examining why so many teenagers with such bright future prospects were taking their own lives in Palo Alto, California. Palo Alto is located in the San Francisco Bay area. Stanford University is located there, and the city is also headquarters to a number of high tech companies including Hewlett Packard, Loral, Tesla Motors, and Ford Research and Innovation Center. Not surprisingly, Palo Alto is one of the wealthiest cities in the country, and its residents are some of the most well-educated.

WE WILL NEVER KNOW HOW MANY CHILDREN
HAVE HAD THEIR LIVES MADE MISERABLE BY BEING
PUSHED TO ACHIEVEMENTS WHICH MAKE THEIR
PARENTS LOOK GOOD.

For this reason, it seems perplexing that in the two high-achieving high schools in Palo Alto, the ten-year suicide rate among their students is four to five times the national average. So many of these suicides are also cluster suicides, which are multiple deaths in close succession and proximity.

Suniya Luther, a psychology professor at Arizona State is quoted in the article and shares her assessment. She says it is not uncommon for children in affluent families to experience a high rate of anxiety and depression. These children feel a great deal of pressure to excel at multiple academic and extracurricular pursuits. They see themselves as cat-astrophically flawed if they don't meet the highest standards of success.

The source of all this pressure begins of course with the parents. One parent asked after a cluster of suicides, "What are we doing to our kids?" Parents are beginning to recognize that they are to blame for putting excessive pressure on their kids to succeed. Unfortunately, they are having a difficult time letting go of their high expectations to achieve because they believe their children's achievements are a reflection on them.

A great shift has taken place in our country. If you go back 100 years, parents focused on their children's character development. To-day the emphasis is placed on their performance, and look at what it is doing to them. This is what pride can do to us and our families.

THE RESULTS OF PRIDE

Tim Keller opens his powerful book, *Counterfeit Gods,* with these chilling words:

> After the global economic crisis began in mid-2008, there followed a tragic string of suicides of formerly wealthy and well-connected individuals. The acting chief financial officer of Freddie Mac, the Federal Home Loan Mortgage Corporation, hanged himself in his basement. The chief executive of Sheldon Good, a leading U.S. real estate auction firm, shot himself in the head behind the wheel of his red Jaguar. A French money manager who invested the wealth of many of Europe's royal and leading families, and who had lost $1.4 billion of his clients' money in Bernard Madoff's Ponzi scheme, slit his wrists and died in his Madison Avenue office. A Danish se-nior executive with HSBC Bank hanged himself in the wardrobe of his 500-a-night suite in Knightsbridge, London. When a Bear Stearns executive learned that he would not be hired by JPMorgan Chase, which had bought his collapsed firm, he took a drug over-dose and leapt from the twenty-ninth floor of his office building.

Most people are quite puzzled over why these talented, well-educated businessmen would take their own lives. The natural response is that they must have been depressed. But why were they depressed?

The answer can be found in one word: shame. They went from being very successful people in the eyes of the world, to being failures, or at least that is the way they saw it. We fear failure because of the shame it generates. Shame is like leukemia of the soul, making us feel as if our lives are worthless and that we do not measure up. Pride devastates clear thinking.

As we have seen, arrogant people seek to be superior to others. Although they believe themselves to be great and powerful, in reality they are crippled with a sense of fear, inferiority, and insecurity. They are extremely needy. They need to feed their egos; they need compliments; they need to be stroked; they need recognition. Though they do not realize it, the proud are actually quite weak, which causes them to be internally filled with shame.

In our culture, we have somehow come to believe that strong men and strong women don't fail. Our definition of a successful person does not include being down and depressed and therefore when people realize they have a problem, they view asking for help as an admission of weakness.

This is what pride will do to us, and yet we cannot see how it affects our lives. Because of our proud hearts, we all fear shame; when we experience it, we retreat into ourselves, trying to protect our image as strong people. There is always that big question that looms in the background: "What are people going to think of me?"

I have known three men fairly well who tragically decided to take their own lives. Looking back, I am amazed at how similar each of their circumstances was. They were all very well liked with great families, yet each of them struggled with the sense that they were failures in the world of business. They each felt that they did not measure up to other men in our community. In the end, each of them felt that they were insignificant, unimportant, and their lives were worthless because of their inability to perform and achieve in the world of business. Clearly, when a person believes their life is worthless, they lose the will to live.

These tragic events were all triggered by the pride of life, and they help me understand why C.S. Lewis said that "pride is the essential vice, the utmost evil. It is the complete anti-God state of mind."

~3~

THE MODERN AGE
OF ARROGANCE

HUMILITY'S STRENGTH IS HIDDEN,
OBSCURED BY OUR BLINDNESS AND THE
AGE OF ARROGANCE IN WHICH WE LIVE.

-David J. Bobb, educator

~ 3 ~

THE MODERN AGE
OF ARROGANCE

rmand Nicholi, a clinical professor of psychiatry at Harvard Medical School, has taught a course at the undergraduate level for 35 years, comparing the beliefs of Sigmund Freud with C.S. Lewis. At the beginning of each semester, he asks his students, "What is your goal in life?" Of course, they all respond that they want to be successful. He then asks, "What does that mean to you?" He has discovered that today students want more than just to make a good living—they all want to be famous.

Our perception of success has changed dramatically. In the present world, we not only want to achieve and accomplish something, but we also want to be well-known and admired for it. Because of the power of television and social media, it is easy to understand the modern obsession with our public image over the desire for private character. Making a good impression is now much more important than doing quality work.

The reason we have become so obsessed with fame and recognition is what the noted historian and former Congressional Librarian Daniel Boorstin calls the "graphic revolution." It started with photography and has evolved to include the television and movie industries, the Internet and digital print media, and most recently, social networking sites such as Facebook, YouTube, Twitter, Instagram, and Snapchat. Boorstin points out that the graphic revolution has created a new kind of power—the power to make even average people doing average things "famous." So much so, he says, that we have now become a culture intensely focused on our becoming celebrities.

BOORSTIN'S PRINCIPLE CONCERN FOR MODERN
SOCIETY IS THAT WE ARE BECOMING MORE IMAGE
CONSCIOUS AND LESS QUALITY CONSCIOUS.

In the past, fame was primarily an honor earned, the result of performing heroic deeds or of making significant contributions to the welfare of the community through inventions, the advancement of education, or industrial strength, to name a few. Boorstin says that today, on the other hand, people are often considered famous simply because they have become well-known through the media. Sports stars, actors and actresses, television personalities and reality stars, and children of celebrities famous for just being children of celebrities are included in this group. The power and allure of fame grows stronger and stronger every day.

Boorstin's principle concern for modern society is that we are becoming more *image* conscious and less *quality* conscious. We give celebrities and the media more and more power over our lives simply because of the images they project rather than the true values they represent. How has this impacted us, particularly as it relates to how we individually respond to the challenges of this new economy?

I don't believe Boorstin is saying that the graphic revolution has changed our legitimate desires to be successful and to contribute to society. To the contrary, I think the problem he points out and underscores for us is that the standards and measures of what constitute that success have changed. This revolution has so transformed our culture that for many in today's society, success now has more to do with public image and the *appearance* of success than it does with the quality of our work and our character. Success today is often divorced from real substance.

Many people are no longer concerned with lives of excellence. Instead, no matter how much a person accomplishes, he does not believe he is successful unless others know about it. We now regard success as achievement *plus* proper recognition of our achievement. The recognition is what makes us feel worthwhile and that we measure up as a success. Christopher Lasch, author of *The Culture of Narcissism*, has perhaps said it best,

> People would rather be envied for their material success than respected for their character.

This is what pride has done to us and it also explains why humility is not of great value in our modern world.

WHERE ARE WE HEADED?

It is hard to believe that 15 years ago, social media was non-existent and yet it now dominates a major part of our lives, particularly with our young people. The great concern is that we are creating a culture of self-admiring narcissists who think the world revolves around them. Social media has become an outlet to self-promote oneself, and its popularity signals that we are becoming a society clearly focused on the glorification of self. For decades people have diligently taken pictures of their loved ones, but in 2013 the word "selfie" was named word of the year by the Oxford English Dictionary.

Keith Campbell is a professor in the psychology department at the University of Georgia. He believes social media is turning our children (tomorrow's adults) into narcissists. He says a 2008 study on narcissism and Facebook discovered evidence that the most narcissistic individuals were those who were more self-promoting on Facebook and had more so-called "friends." He goes on to say narcissists thrive in an environment where there are shallow relationships and many opportunities to promote yourself.

A very good book was written about our modern narcissistic culture back in 2010, entitled *The Narcissism Epidemic*, and was co-authored by psychologists Dr. Campbell and Dr. Jean Twenge. In their extensive research, they compiled evidence that was both compelling and appalling. As you read through the text, you find at the heart of narcissism is pride and arrogance. It is, therefore, not surprising that they recognized a dark side of narcissism that leads to suffering. The symptoms are very destructive to one's own personal well-being and to others as well.

According to Twenge and Campbell,

> Narcissists brag about their achievements (while blaming others for their shortcomings), focus on their physical appearance, value material goods that display status . . . constantly turn the conversation back to themselves, manipulate and cheat to get ahead, surround themselves with people who look up to them (like a "posse" or entourage), seek out "Trophy partners" who make them look good and jump at opportunities to garner attention and fame.

Clearly, this is not the way to make friends and endear yourselves to people, but narcissists are simply not aware of their arrogance or of other people.

APPEARING TO BE PERFECT

People who yearn for validation on social media have developed an obsession to hide all their flaws (which they assume to be unacceptable and unattractive) behind some kind of appearance that will impress viewers and be much more pleasing. In real life, the people who surround you see how flawed and imperfect you are. However, the appearance of perfection can easily be maintained on social media by creating an impressive appearance that is not real.

Sociologist Donna Freitas discusses this in her wonderful book, *The Happiness Effect; How Social Media Is Driving a Generation to Appear Perfect at Any Cost.* She did most of her research through interviewing 200 college students at 13 universities. She concluded that all these students are driven to appear to be perfectly happy, all the time. They all have a compulsion to present themselves as successful people who are totally happy. It is unthinkable for them to appear to be anything else.

PRIDE BEGINS WHEN YOU COMPARE
YOURSELF TO OTHERS.

Freitas sees that their problem is the same one that all people have who are full of pride and arrogance. They cannot be transparent and vulnerable with anyone since they cannot discuss their inadequacies, struggles, and fears. If they did, they would not be a person who is happy and who has their act together. People today are more concerned with *appearing* to be happy than actually *being* happy. How you appear is everything.

Freitas states these young adults are consistently comparing themselves on social media. Pride begins when you compare yourself with others. Freitas says it becomes a "24/7 sport, with pictures, profiles and status updates displaying legions of happy people having amazing experiences alongside beautiful girlfriends and handsome boyfriends." Unfortunately, they are not truly happy and end up suffering alone in isolation, for rarely would one ever post the truth and reveal that they are sad or depressed.

LIVING IN AN AGE OF ARROGANCE

We live in a time where competing, succeeding, and winning the applause and admiration of others becomes all-consuming. Modern culture teaches us to promote and glorify ourselves as we compete out in the marketplace, hardly ever receiving any encouragement to be humble and unpretentious.

Life has not always been this way. In his outstanding book; *The Road to Character*, David Brooks confronts this transformation that has taken place in our country.

On Sunday evenings my local NPR station rebroadcasts old radio programs. A few years ago I was driving home and heard a program called *Command Performance*, which was a variety show that went out to the troops during World War II. The episode I happened to hear was broadcast the day after V-J Day, on August 15, 1945.

The episode featured some of the era's biggest celebrities: Frank Sinatra, Marlene Dietrich, Cary Grant, Bette Davis, and many others. But the most striking feature of the show was its tone of self-effacement and humility. The Allies had just completed one of the noblest military victories in human history. And yet there was no chest beating. Nobody was erecting triumphal arches.

"Well, it looks like this is it," the host, Bing Crosby, opened. "What can you say at a time like this? You can't throw your skimmer in the air. That's for run-of-the-mill holidays. I guess all anybody can do is thank God it's over." The mezzo-soprano Risë Stevens came on and sang a solemn version of "Ave Maria," and then Crosby came back on to summarize the mood: "Today, though, our deep-down feeling is one of humility."

That sentiment was repeated throughout the broadcast. The actor Burgess Meredith read a passage written by Ernie Pyle, the war correspondent. Pyle had been killed just a few months before, but he had written an article anticipating what victory would mean: "We won this war because our men are brave and because of many other things—because of Russia, England, and China and the passage of time and the gift of nature's materials. We did not win it because destiny created us better than all other people. I hope that in victory we are more grateful than proud."

I arrived home before the program was over and listened to that radio show in my driveway for a time. Then I went inside and turned on a football game. A quarterback threw a short pass to a wide receiver, who was tackled almost immediately for a two-yard gain. The defensive player did what all professional athletes do these days in moments of personal accomplishments. He did a self-puffing victory dance, as the camera lingered.

It occurred to me that I had just watched more self-celebration after a two-yard gain than I had heard after the United States won World War II.

This incident triggered something in the mind of David Brooks, as he recognized that this shift in reality symbolized a shift in our own culture, a shift from a culture that was once humble and grateful to a culture of arrogance and self-promotion. It made him realize that this "was like a doorway into the different ways it is possible to live in this world."

This realization led Brooks into researching and collecting data that proves we have experienced a broad shift from a culture of humility to what he calls the culture "of the Big Me." He says that we were once a country that encouraged people to think humbly of themselves to a culture that now encourages people to see themselves as "the center of the universe."

This in fact may explain the current state of our nation.

~ 4 ~

A MODERN
PARABLE

"TWO DIFFERENT CHARACTERS ARE PRESENTED
TO OUR EMULATION: THE ONE, OF PROUD
AMBITION AND OSTENTATIOUS AVIDITY. THE
OTHER, OF HUMBLE MODESTY AND EQUITABLE
JUSTICE. TWO DIFFERENT MODELS, TWO
DIFFERENT PICTURES, ARE HELD OUT TO US,
ACCORDING TO WHICH WE MAY FASHION
OUR OWN CHARACTER AND BEHAVIOR; THE
ONE MORE GAUDY AND GLITTERING IN ITS
COLOURING; THE OTHER MORE CORRECT AND
MORE EXQUISITELY BEAUTIFUL IN ITS OUTLINE."

- Adam Smith, Scottish economist and author

~ 4 ~

A MODERN PARABLE

Steven and Samuel Chamberlain were identical twin brothers, born in 1965. They grew up in Memphis, Tennessee, and were inseparable. They both were serious students and great athletes. Steven was the quarterback on their high school football team, while Samuel was the team's star receiver. In the spring they both played baseball.

Though it was a difficult decision, they decided to attend different colleges. Steven enrolled at the University of North Carolina, and Samuel went to Wake Forest. The four years flew by and both young men flourished socially and academically. It was during their senior years that they both were notified that they had been accepted into the Vanderbilt School of Medicine. It was a dream come true.

Medical school was difficult and the hours were long, but the two brothers excelled in their school work and training. Steven Chamberlain became a well-known orthopedic surgeon and Samuel a very well-respected vascular surgeon. They both moved back to Memphis and began their medical practices. As the years went by they married, had children, and remained very close. Both of their families eventually moved to a very fine suburb called Mountain Ridge. The two families lived just down the street from each other. Life was good.

One day Steven received a call from one of his patients. This particular patient was a very distinguished realtor in their community, and he revealed to Steven, confidentially, that he had just been given the listing on a piece of the most coveted land in Mountain Ridge. It was one hundred acres of choice property on top of the small mountain for which the community was named.

Steven realized he could build his dream home on this property, and he would have an incredible view of the community below. It would be a showplace that everyone in Mountain Ridge could look up to and see. Within an hour, he had spoken to his wife and they made the offer at list price.

News that this choice piece of property had been sold spread quickly throughout the community. Everyone was curious to see the magnificent house that would be built upon the hill.

It took over two years for the house to be constructed; once it was finished, it was captivating, particularly at night when it was all lit up.

It was an 8,000 square foot house with seven bedrooms and ten bathrooms. It had an indoor and outdoor pool, tennis courts, and a stable for their daughter's horses. When the couple decided to have a big gala to allow people in the community to see their new home, everyone was anxious over whether they would be invited or not.

Every morning Steven woke up and walked out on one of his balconies with a cup of coffee and the Wall Street Journal in hand and looked down on the town below. Without realizing it, he gloated, knowing that he lived in the nicest home in Mountain Ridge and probably all of Memphis. He reasoned to himself that he had worked hard for it and therefore clearly deserved the beautiful place.

Also every morning, Samuel woke up down in the suburbs below. He too sipped on a cup of coffee on his modest backyard porch where he had a perfect view of his brother's beautiful home. He thought to himself, "That pompous, arrogant brother of mine. He is so full of himself." He thought about his own life and gloated over the fact that he had a much more modest lifestyle than his brother and could therefore give more money to the church and to charity. He also reflected on the fact that his children were not nearly as spoiled as his brother's, who were real brats. He was very proud of his wise choices and good works as he compared his life and family with those of his brother.

✦ ✦ ✦

In this parable you find both of these brothers are guilty of pride. The first brother, Steven, was comparing his possession and material wealth to everyone else's in the community. It caused him to have a feeling of superiority over them.

He was guilty of what so many of us are guilty of—"conspicuous consumption," a term coined back in 1899 by Thorstein Veblen in his book, *The Theory of the Leisure Class*. Conspicuous consumption is when you buy something, not primarily for its usefulness, but for the way it makes you look in the eyes of others. Veblen shared the following message:

> People above the line of base subsistence, in this age and all earlier ages, do not use the surplus, which society has given them, primarily for useful purposes. They do not seek to expand their own lives, to live more wisely, intelligently, understandingly, but to impress other people with the fact that they have a surplus . . . spending money, time and effort quite uselessly in the pleasurable business of inflating the ego.

Though we may not realize it, there is a psychological fulfillment that comes from being envied by others. Veblen contended that it is possible to persuade people to buy products that are not particularly superior in quality by heavily publicizing the fact that the products are expensive. And so he came up with the term conspicuous consumption, meaning that people buy costly items, not because they are of higher quality, but because the possession displays to others how rich the owners are.

Veblen shows us how pride is so often the motive behind our decision to make purchases that enable us to proclaim to the world we are wealthy. Steven was guilty of pride, and it was quite obvious, and the entire community could see it.

It is important to recognize that pride emanates from a multitude of sources: wealth, achievement, power, beauty, and knowledge. However, there is a pride that Reinhold Niebuhr believed is the most dangerous—the pride of virtue, or what the Bible calls self-righteousness. In the four Gospels, you see Jesus' most searing words aimed at the Pharisees and their self-righteousness. It is the one sin that quickly brings forth His anger.

Self-righteousness is what Samuel is guilty of. It is important to notice how comparison is again at work. He compares himself to his brother who lives up on the hill. He compares their lifestyles and concludes that his is morally superior, and naturally presumes that he is so much more righteous than his brother.

What I find to be so interesting is that through comparison, each of these men is guilty of pride. However, pride that results in conspicuous consumption is easy to detect when someone is trying to impress you. I remember a college classmate who rode the technology boom to great wealth. He built an unbelievably large, beautiful home. It was a real showplace. Several years later, he abruptly sold the house. The reason he gave: "I built this house for all the wrong reasons. I was trying to make a statement to the world that I was successful." He eventually saw the pride in his life.

The problem with self-righteousness is that it is so difficult to see because you are blinded by your own perceived goodness. In Samuel's mind, all he could see was the good he was doing. "I am living modestly; I am giving money away; I am doing so much good for the community, unlike my extravagant, pompous brother." This is a picture of putting yourself in the place of God as judge, and in the process you are blinded by your presumptuousness.

THE END OF THE STORY

Five years went by, and one day Samuel received a call from Steven. He immediately could tell that something was terribly wrong. His brother was weeping over the phone. Steven finally was able to get the words out, "My wife is having an affair and is leaving me. She is going to take me to the cleaners. We are going to have to put our property on the market." He was clearly devastated. After getting over the shock, Samuel remarked how sorry he was to hear the news and to let him know if there was anything he could do. He finished the conversation by telling his brother he would be praying for him.

As he hung up the phone, Samuel smiled. He was secretly rejoicing over his brother's misfortune. His first thought was that his brother was getting what he deserved because "God is opposed to the proud." Over the coming weeks and months, Samuel outwardly displayed sadness and grief over Steven's difficult circumstances. However, inwardly he reveled over his brother's troubles, somehow believing he was personally being vindicated for living such a good and righteous life. This is pride.

The well-known Southern writer Walker Percy is known for his peculiar talent in exploring the deeper questions of modern life relating to our habits, our self-deceptiveness, our fears, and our complexity. In one of his books, a spoof of modern life, entitled *Lost in the Cosmos: The Last Self-Help Book*, Percy offers a humorous take on modern Western culture's obsession with pop psychology, which offers simple, untested answers to life's most difficult questions. In the book, Percy gives a number of multiple choice tests as a reflection of the self-help quizzes that are so popular in many successful consumer self-help books and magazines. The questions are full of moral challenges, often highlighted in humorous patterns, one of which I will paraphrase:

> It is early morning and you are standing in front of your home, reading the headlines of the local newspaper. Your neighbor of five years, Charlie, comes out to get his paper. You look at him sympathetically—he doesn't take good care of himself and you know that he has been having severe chest pains and is facing coronary by-pass surgery. But he is not acting like a cardiac patient this morning!

He jogs over in his sweat pants, all smiles. He has triple good news! "My chest pains," he crows, "turned out to be nothing more than a hiatal hernia, nothing serious." He has also just gotten word of a great promotion he has received and that he and his family will soon be moving to a new home, which happens to be in a much more exclusive part of town. Then, after a pause, he warbles on, "Now I can afford to buy the lake house we have always dreamed of owning."

Once this news settles in, you respond, "That is great, Charlie. I'm very happy for you."

Now, please fill in the following multiple choice. There is only one correct answer to each question.

Question: Are you truly happy for Charlie?

a. Yes, you are thrilled for Charlie; you could not be any happier for him and his family.

b. If the truth be known, you really don't feel so great about Charlie's news. It's good news for Charlie, certainly, but it's not good news for you.

Percy then gives the following directions:

If your answer to the question above is b, please specify the nature of your dissatisfaction. Do the following thought experiment—which of the following alternative scenarios concerning Charlie would make you feel better?

a. You go out to get your paper a few days later, and you hear from another neighbor that Charlie has undergone a quadruple coronary bypass and may not make it.

b. Charlie does not have heart trouble, but he did not get his promotion.

c. As the two of you are standing in front of your homes, Charlie has a heart attack, and you save his life by pounding his chest and giving him mouth-to-mouth resuscita-

tion, turning his triple good news into quadruple good
news. How happy would that make you?

d.   Charlie is dead.

Percy then asks:

Just how much good news about Charlie can you tolerate?

Percy uses this exercise to flush out the desires of the heart. He wants
to show us how our pride causes us to consistently compare ourselves
with others. I am reminded again of C.S. Lewis's words that pride
is like a spiritual cancer that eats up the possibility of us ever being
content with our lives. Percy shows us how the pride of our hearts is
the reason for our discontentment.

THE DEVASTATION OF PRIDE

Over the years I have wondered what the ultimate extent of pride's
devastation is to people's lives and relationships. In these first four
chapters we have seen how its consequences can cascade through our
lives. It creates incredible instability, fear, and weakness. Since we
cannot detect pride in the depths of our hearts, we never really know
what is wrong with us.

This is why humility is of great value. Stephen Covey said, "Humility truly is the mother of all virtues. It makes us a vessel, a vehicle,
an agent instead of 'the source' or the principle. It unleashes all other
learning, all growth and process." Humility is the place of growth
and strength.

This is at the heart of life's greatest paradox. You would never
expect the strongest, most influential, and most inspiring people to
be humble. As author John Dickson has observed, you would never
expect true greatness to go hand in hand with a virtue that, on its
face, would appear to curb achievement and stifle your ability to influence. Yet, that is the great paradox. *There is power in the humble life.*

~ 5 ~

UNDERSTANDING
THE
HUMBLE LIFE

I KNOW HOW GREAT IS THE EFFORT
NEEDED TO CONVINCE THE PROUD OF THE
POWER AND EXCELLENCE OF HUMILITY,
AN EXCELLENCE WHICH MAKES IT SOAR
ABOVE THE SUMMITS OF THIS WORLD.

- *Augustine, theologian and philosopher*

~ 5 ~

UNDERSTANDING
THE HUMBLE LIFE

Being humble is not something that comes naturally to us as human beings. I have found that most people do not really know what humility looks like. Historically, humility has been linked to the word meekness. In the Beatitudes we hear Jesus say, "Blessed are the meek, for they shall inherit the earth." Of course, meekness rhymes with weakness, so who in the world would possibly want to be meek? I have never heard a father say, "I want my son to grow up and be meek."

The word "meekness" surprisingly comes from the word *praus*, which is a powerful animal that knows how to restrain its power. The idea here is that meek and humble people are powerful people, though they do not flaunt their strength and power.

I think it is important to note that since C.S. Lewis said that pride is the anti-God state of mind, it is only logical that humility is seeking God's mindset and His view of life. If Lewis is correct when he says that pride leads to every other vice, then humility must be the root of all virtues. Without understanding God's place in the universe, there really is no way for us to understand humility.

Famous skeptic Friedrich Nietzsche loathed Christianity because he believed it was for weak people. He hated the way the God of the Bible took such an offense at the pride of man. He believed the Christian attack on pride was to mask the weakness of humility in the Christian faith.

The great theologian John Stott responds with these powerful words:

At no point does the Christian mind come into more violent collision with the secular mind than in its insistence on humility, with all the weakness it entails. The wisdom of the world values power, not humility. We have drunk in more of the power philosophy of Friedrich Nietzsche than we realize. Nietzsche dreamed of the rise of a daring ruler race. Tough, masculine, and oppressive Nietzsche worshipped power. He despised Jesus for His weakness. The ideal of Nietzsche was the Übermensch, the superman, but the ideal of Jesus was the little child. There is no possibility of compromise between these two images; we are obliged to choose.

C.S. Lewis says that in God, we encounter something that is immeasurably superior to ourselves. In his book, *Guide to Humility*, Thomas Jones says,

> Humility is so right because it so squares with reality. It is a reality that we owe other people a great deal. Now consider an even deeper reality. There is a God and you are not Him. There is a great and awesome God who created the Heavens and the Earth and you are not Him. There is a God who knows all, and understands all, and is in control of all, and you are not Him. And I am not Him. He is God, and we are not. He is the great God, and you and I are small people. Very small in comparison to Him.

I find it interesting what Jones says about being in control. Many people keep God at a safe distance because they do not want Him to interfere with their lives. They do not in any way want to give up control of their lives. However, you have to wonder, do we really have that much control over anything?

For instance:

- *Did you have any control over when and where you were born?*

- *Did you have any control over the color of your skin, your eyes, your hair, your height?*

- *Do you have any control over your talents, your abilities, or your intelligence?*

- *Do you have any control over the economy, the stock market, interest rates, or the deficit?*

- *Although we try to live healthy lives, do we have control over getting cancer or Alzheimer's, or having a stroke?*

- *As my children get older and become more independent, I am realizing that soon I will have little or no control over them. They will be making their own decisions and choices.*

- *Do we have control over the aging process?*

- *In all probability, we will have no control over how and when we die.*

- *Finally, when we do die, we experience the loss of every earthly thing we gained in this life.*

So, are we really in control of much of anything?

We don't seem to recognize this, or at least have not given it much thought. We are not in control. We are weak creatures; our bodies are wasting away, which in itself should cause us to see our great need for God. Only when we understand our need for Him does true humility begin. As Andrew Murray puts it, "Humility, the place of entire dependence on God, is the first duty of the creature and is the root of every good human quality."

Pride seeks to be independent of God. At its heart, the pride we speak of is spiritual. Søren Kierkegaard, the famous Danish philosopher, observed that we all suffer from spiritual pride. We think we can accomplish great things, achieve prosperity, and find a purpose that is big enough to discover meaning in life, and do all of this without God. The prideful heart of man causes him to believe, "I do not need God."

I am reminded of a conversation I had with a good friend several years ago. His father was a very wealthy, self-made man and had built a large, successful business on his own. One day my friend approached his father and shared his concern that his father had no spiritual life. His father responded, "What do I need God for? I have everything I need." You can see why C.S. Lewis calls pride "the anti-God state of mind."

I do not know if this man ever changed his mind, but a few years after he had made this declaration of not needing God, he died. Over time, life has a way of humbling us all.

GOD'S POINT OF VIEW

I think it is significant that God has such high regard for the humble, and such great contempt against the proud.

In the Old Testament, in Isaiah 2:12-17 we are told:

For the Lord of Hosts will have a day of reckoning against everyone who is proud and lofty, against everyone who is lifted up, that he may be abased. And it will be against all the cedars of Lebanon that are lofty and lifted up, against all the oaks of Bashan, against every high tower, against every fortified wall, against all the ships of Tarsus, and against all the beautiful craft. The pride of man will be humbled, and the loftiness of men will be abased, and the Lord alone will be exalted in that day.

In Proverbs 16:5,

Everyone who is proud in heart is an abomination to the Lord; assuredly, he will not go unpunished.

There is also a phrase that you see several times in the New Testament, that God is "opposed to the proud." Seeing that God is totally against those who are proud and arrogant and that it is an abomination in His sight should get our attention.

On the other hand, it is quite clear that God has special regard and honor for the humble. We are told:

Oh, Lord, You have heard the desire of the humble. You will strengthen their heart. You will incline Your ear (Psalm 10:17).

He leads the humble in justice. He teaches the humble His way (Psalm 25:9).

When pride comes, then comes dishonor, but, with the humble, there is wisdom (Proverbs 11:2).

A man's pride will bring him low, but a humble spirit will obtain honor (Proverbs 29:23).

Humble yourselves in the presence of the Lord and He will exalt you (James 4:10).

Humble yourselves therefore under the mighty hand of God, that He may exalt you at the proper time (1 Peter 5:6).

And then most significantly, in both James 4:16 and 1 Peter 5:5, we are told that "God gives grace to the humble." Under no other circumstances does He ever promise to give His grace—only to the humble. This is a very significant promise.

Grace is a word that is often misunderstood and literally means receiving God's favor. The most common definition used in the Bible is the unmerited favor of God, which applies to salvation. But in the New Testament, the word "grace" is most commonly applied to living this life with God's power—a divine enablement. Through grace, God enables us to do that which we cannot do ourselves (Hebrews 13:9; 2 Timothy 2:1). Grace is incredibly significant. God gives His strength and power only to the humble through grace. This, of course, is the theme of this book: "the power of a humble life."

WHO GETS THE CREDIT

Pride is not only competitive in nature but causes us to gloat because we feel superior to those with whom we compare ourselves. We can take all the credit for our success. It is like the saying, "He was born on third base but somehow thinks he hit a triple."

Pride looks at life and takes credit for all the good things. Pride says, "I accomplished it; I worked harder than everyone else; I deserve it, and therefore I should receive all the glory."

Tim Keller says that pride claims to be the author of everything good we do and accomplish. Therefore we believe we deserve all the credit. He says it is a form of cosmic plagiarism, where you have been given something as a gift but then you take all the credit for it and say, "I did it; it is my work."

In the Old Testament, Moses said that arrogance is looking at your life, your abilities, and your achievements, and thinking in your heart that it is *your* strength, *your* power, and *your* ability that has led to all your success. Humility helps you to recognize that all you are and all you have is a gift from God and a result of other people contributing to your life. Read the following example from Drayton Nabers, Jr.'s book, *The Case for Character*:

> Let's take the example of a tailback who wins the Heisman Trophy. This Heisman winner gets his name in the paper and his face on ESPN. But where did he get the DNA that created the strong body? And where did he get the great coordination that helped him win the prize? How many of the one hundred trillion cells in his body did he create?
>
> We are told that for each of these cells there is a bank of instructions more detailed than the thirty-two volumes of the *Encyclopedia Britannica* put together. Does this tailback understand even one of these instructions? (For that matter, does even the smartest doctor or biologist in the world fully understand the marvel of a single human cell?)
>
> "But I worked so hard," the tailback might say. "I went to the weight room. I practiced harder than anyone else on the team."
>
> To him we could reply: "But who taught you to work that hard? Who built the weight room? Who bought the equipment?

Who built the university, including the stadium you played in? Who cut the grass there and laid out the lines and boundaries? Did you hire or pay your coaches? Did you recruit your team-mates? Did you open up those holes in the line that you ran through?

If this tailback has humility, he will express nothing but over-flowing gratitude when he wins the Heisman—to his parents, to his teachers, to his coaches, to all the players on his team, to everyone who helped him along the way. Most of all, time and time again, he will express gratitude to God.

In describing humility, Nabers states:

> . . . humility is a form of wisdom. It is thinking clearly. It is simply being realistic. It is knowing who really deserves the credit and the glory for what we do.

This ageless thought says it all: "We drink from wells we did not dig and we are warmed by fires we did not build" (Deuteronomy 6:11). In this light, humility is only logical.

I often share a powerful, true story in my speeches because it enables us to see the clear contrast between pride and humility. The story comes from Stephen K. Scott's book, *The Richest Man Who Ever Lived.*

> My former church pastor, Dr. Jim Borror, while visiting a church in the Northwest, was asked by a woman to meet with her husband, a multimillionaire entrepreneur with thousands of employees. Although this man had tens of millions of dollars and everything money could buy, he was unhappy, bitter, and cantankerous. No one liked being around him, and contention and strife followed him wherever he went. He was disliked by his employees and even his children. His wife barely tolerated him.
>
> When he met the man, Dr. Borror listened to him talk about his accomplishments and quickly realized that pride ruled this man's heart and mind. He claimed he had single-handedly built his company from scratch. Even his parents hadn't given him a

dime. He had worked his way through college.

Jim said, "So you did everything by yourself."

"Yep," the man replied.

Jim repeated, "No one ever gave you anything."

"Nothing!"

So Jim asked, "Who changed your diapers? Who fed you as a baby? Who taught you how to read and write? Who gave you your first job after college? Who serves food in your company's cafeteria? Who cleans the toilets in your company's rest rooms?" The man hung his head in shame. Moments later, with tears in his eyes, he said, "Now that I think about it, I haven't accomplished anything by myself. Without the kindness and efforts of others, I probably wouldn't have anything." Jim nodded and asked, "Don't you think they deserve a little thanks?"

That man's heart was transformed, seemingly overnight. In the months that followed, he wrote thank-you letters to every person he could think of who had made a contribution to his life. He wrote thank-you notes to every one of his 3,000 employees. He not only felt a deep sense of gratitude, he began to treat everyone around him with respect and appreciation.

When Dr. Borror visited him a year or two later, he could hardly recognize him. Happiness and peace had replaced the anger and contention in his heart. He looked years younger. His employees loved him for treating them with the honor and respect that true humility engenders.

In this story you see the dark side of arrogance and what it can do to a person's life and relationships. This man was disliked by everyone with whom he came into contact. Most significantly, he took all the credit for their contributions to his accomplishments. Clearly he had no awareness of the pride that ruled his heart and mind.

Once he had been wisely confronted by Dr. Borror, a major transformation took place in his life. As he began to give people the proper credit that was due them, everything changed. Not only did it impact the relationships he had with others, but it transformed this man's life. *There is power in the humble life.*

~6~

THE ESSENCE OF HUMILITY AND ITS POWER

A MAN'S PRIDE WILL BRING HIM LOW,
BUT A HUMBLE SPIRIT WILL OBTAIN HONOR.

—Proverbs 29:23

~ 6 ~

THE ESSENCE OF
HUMILITY AND ITS POWER

Let's continue to examine the essence of humility and better understand the nature of its power by looking at some real life examples.

A number of years ago, Jim Collins, who was a faculty member at the Stanford University Graduate School of Business, wrote a best-selling book entitled, *Built to Last*. It was based on a management study of companies that he and his associates made back in the 1990s with the intent of analyzing and demonstrating how great companies sustain themselves over time.

In studying the data, Collins came up with the idea of trying to determine if certain universal characteristics distinguished truly great companies. Using tough benchmarks, Collins and his research team identified eleven elite companies doing such a good job that they produced phenomenal results for fifteen consecutive years (some of these companies included Abbott Labs, Kimberly Clark, and Nucor Steel). He and his team sought to determine how these companies made the leap from merely being *good* companies to becoming *great* companies. He took the results of all this intensive research and wrote what would come to be one of the best-selling business books ever published, *Good to Great*.

What I find interesting is that Collins gave his research team explicit instructions to downplay the role of top executives. He did not believe that the business community needed another book on leadership. Although he had insisted they ignore the role of the company executives, the research team kept pushing back. They soon came to recognize something very unusual about the executives in these good-to-great companies.

The debate between Collins and his team went back and forth until, as Collins put it, "the data won." They recognized that all the executives from these good-to-great companies were cut from the same cloth. They all were what he called "Level 5 Leaders."

Collins wrote, "Level 5 Leaders are a study in duality: modest and willful, humble and fearless." These good-to-great leaders never desired to be celebrities or to be lifted up on a pedestal. Collins declared that they were "seemingly ordinary people quietly producing extraordinary results." What Collins and his team of researchers clearly observed is that a Level 5 Leader builds enduring greatness through the paradoxical blend of personal humility and professional will.

Collins points out how so many leaders are very prideful, driven by big egos. Their main concern is their own personal greatness. Their great desire is to be business celebrities. He says they often fail to set up the company for future success because they reason, what greater testament to your own personal greatness than to see the business flounder once you are gone.

Tim Keller makes a similar observation when he says, "The humble are kind and gentle, but also brave and fearless. If you are to be humble, you cannot have one without the other." You see this attitude in a number of the great leaders in the Bible. John the Baptist is a great example. When John's disciples were complaining that all the people were leaving him to follow Jesus, John made it clear that Jesus must increase and that he must decrease. On the other hand, you see John courageously confront King Herod about how corrupt he was to take Herodias, his brother's wife, to be his own unlawful wife. It landed him in jail and eventually cost him his life.

The Apostle Paul considered himself to be the chief of all sinners and openly shared his struggles, yet boldly went into the streets of Athens and Rome to proclaim the gospel.

One of my favorite examples of true humility in a man is found in Numbers 12:3 where we learn that Moses was the most humble man on the face of the earth. Yet we see Moses go before the most powerful

RESEARCHERS FOR THE BOOK *GOOD TO GREAT*
RECOGNIZED THAT ALL THE EXECUTIVES
FROM THE GOOD-TO-GREAT COMPANIES WERE CUT
FROM THE SAME CLOTH. THEY WERE ALL . . . "MODEST
AND WILLFUL, HUMBLE AND FEARLESS." (JIM COLLINS)

man on earth at the time—Pharaoh, king of Egypt—who could have easily had him killed if he so desired. Moses boldly stood before Pharaoh and said to him in essence, "I want you to let my people go. I want you to give up your entire slave labor force, the key to your entire economic and military superiority. I want you to do it without payment. And I don't want you to mess around; I want you to do it quickly."

Clearly, strength is found in the humble life. The humble don't make decisions by sticking their fingers in the air to see what other people think. They enjoy a fortitude and an inner strength that comes only through God's grace. They know who they are. Their lives are not consumed by trying to please and impress others.

PICTURES OF STRENGTH AND THE HUMBLE LIFE

We can easily theorize about life and how it works. I think at this point, we have already seen how pride and arrogance are deadly in a person's life. It can have devastating consequences, and we can be oblivious to its presence in our lives, until we get burned by it. Unfortunately, the final outcome can lead to circumstances that are irreparable.

Humility, however, is not something that modern people value or pursue. It is natural to be skeptical when you hear the phrase: "The power of a humble life," so I am going to give you a number of examples that will help you see what happens in real life when one possesses the precious gift of humility.

✦ ✦ ✦

Dr. Armand Nicholi, author of the book, *The Question of God*, developed great insight into the life of C.S. Lewis through his research on the man. Lewis was an atheist through the first 31 years of his life, and during this period he always dreamed of being famous. In an essay that he wrote in 1941, he speaks of dreams of success and fame, hoping one day the world would acknowledge what a remarkable person he was. Before Lewis' conversion to Christianity, Nicholi says that he was proud and arrogant as were many who attended the elite boarding schools and prestigious universities in England. Lewis writes of his experiences at school:

> I have never seen a community so competitive, so full of snobbery and flunkeyism, a ruling class so selfish and so class conscious, or a proletariat so fawning.

Shortly before becoming a Christian, Lewis began to examine his life for the first time, and he didn't like what he saw. He had often thought of how clever he was as a teacher and dreamed of being admired by his students. He also yearned to be a well-known writer. Yet, when he became a Christian, Lewis seemed to forget about himself and his desire for fame. Ironically, that is when he found it. Nicholi says,

> He found that when he concentrated on writing and forgot about becoming famous as a writer, he both wrote well and became recognized for it. This may have contributed to his oft-repeated principle that when first things are put first, second things don't decrease, they increase.

Lewis's desire for fame began to really diminish because he realized how it posed such a great danger. He saw very clearly that it was nothing more than the desire to be more well-known than others, and such a desire was rooted in pride.

Lewis matured as a Christian and became more alert to the presence of pride in his own life. Twelve years before he died, he wrote in a letter:

> I am now in my fiftieth year. I feel my zeal for writing, and whatever talent I originally possessed, to be decreasing; nor (I believe) do I please my readers as I used to . . . Perhaps it will be the most wholesome thing for my soul that I lose both fame and skill lest I were to fall into that evil disease, vainglory.

What is ironic is that Lewis produced some of his greatest books over those next twelve years.

At the end of his life, he believed his work was done, he had fulfilled his role and exerted about as much influence as he ever would. A week before his death he told his brother Warren, "I have done all that I was sent into the world to do, and I am ready to go."

He never dreamed he would become the best-selling Christian author to ever live!

ESPN and *Sports Illustrated* call Coach John Wooden the greatest coach of the 20th century. His stats bear that out. In 40 years of coaching, he compiled an 885-203 record—a winning percentage of .813. His historic tenure as coach of the UCLA Bruins, which spanned 27 years, included four 30-0 seasons, an 88-game winning streak, and ten national championships—seven of those in a row (1966-1973). And he is one of only two people enshrined in the Basketball Hall of Fame as both a player and a coach.

As I have researched the life of John Wooden, every source I read pointed to his humility as the key to his success. Wooden was wary of recognition and fame because he understood that pride was dangerous and could easily ruin a player or a team.

Dr. Ronald Riggio, a psychologist who specializes in leadership, wrote an article in the publication *Psychology Today* about the leadership of John Wooden. He writes that the first lesson to be learned from the life of Coach Wooden is to be humble. Coaching was not about the coach, for Wooden it was all about the development of student athletes. Riggio had the opportunity to speak with Coach Wooden and was surprised when the coach told him how much he loved Division III college basketball where the players are not on scholarship but play simply for the love of the game. Later Wooden told him, "I think if I had to do it over again, I would have coached Division III." Riggio was stunned that the greatest coach ever in collegiate sports said he would give away all the glory he received for the "love of the game."

Pat Williams, who wrote a book on the life of Wooden says that people like Coach Wooden are rare. They are greatly admired and praised by others, but they seem to be unaware of their own greatness. Williams also seemed to think that Coach Wooden had what those level 5 leaders had and what Jim Collins wrote about in *Good to Great*—a paradoxical blend of personal humility and professional will. In describing Wooden, Williams said he modeled the perfect balance of confidence and humility. In his own words, Coach Wooden said,

Confidence must be monitored so that it does not spoil or rot and turn into arrogance. I have never gone into a game assuming victory. All opponents have been respected, none feared. I taught those under my supervision to do the same. This reflects confidence, not arrogance. Arrogance will bring you down by your own hands.

"TALENT IS GOD-GIVEN; BE HUMBLE. FAME IS MAN-GIVEN; BE GRATEFUL. CONCEIT IS SELF-GIVEN; BE CAREFUL." (JOHN WOODEN)

Pat Williams believes that the outcome of John Wooden's life can be boiled down to this simple equation: "Confidence plus humility is the simple formula to greatness." Williams went on to say, "Who is Coach Wooden? He is a guy who never sought out the limelight. He was always trying to stay behind the scenes. He never cared about receiving accolades for his coaching; it was all about the team."

One of the greatest quotes of John Wooden is very simple but quite profound: "Talent is God-given; be humble. Fame is man-given; be grateful. Conceit is self-given; be careful."

◆ ◆ ◆

When Dwight Eisenhower left office after two terms as President of the United States, I was seven years old. I never knew much about him until I read David Brooks wonderful book, *The Road to Character*.

Ike, as he was often affectionately called, graduated from West Point in the class of 1915. Though he lived in the shadow of World War I, he never saw military action or left the United States. When he finally received orders to be shipped out, the war had already ended.

In 1918 Ike was promoted to lieutenant colonel and would not receive another promotion for 20 years. After World War I there was a glut of officers and therefore not many opportunities for advancement. Ike did not receive his first star as a general until he was fifty-one; and as time went by, no one expected great things from him.

Anyone who has studied Eisenhower's life will recognize that his humble approach to life in the military is what propelled him to such great heights. Although he was not rising in the ranks as I am sure he would have wanted, he submitted his own desires for the sake of the military. His memoirs reveal that he learned and accepted "the basic lesson of the military—the proper place for a soldier is where he is ordered by his superiors." Over the years, there was nothing glamorous about his career; he was just given run-of-the-mill-assignments.

David Brooks gives some great insight into Ike's humble approach to life in the military.

As a staff officer—never a coveted or glamorous role—Eisenhower learned to master procedure, process, teamwork, and organization. He learned the secrets of thriving within the organization.

"When I go to a new station I look to see who is the strongest and ablest man on the post. I forget my own ideas and do everything in my power to promote what he says is right."

He also gained a perspective on himself. He began carrying around an anonymous little poem:

> Take a bucket, fill it with water,
> Put your hand in—clear up to the wrist.
> Now pull it out; the hole that remains
> Is a measure of how much you'll be missed . . .
>
> The moral of this quaint example:
> To do just the best that you can,
> Be proud of yourself, but remember,
> There is no indispensable Man!

The individual who had the greatest impact on Eisenhower and who served as a great example of the humble life was Fox Connor. He served as the ideal humble leader, and from him Ike learned the great maxim, "Always take your job seriously, never yourself."

Eisenhower would later write in reference to Connor:

> A sense of humility is a quality I have observed in every leader whom I have deeply admired. My own conviction is that every leader should have enough humility to accept, publicly, the responsibility for the mistakes of the subordinates he has himself selected and, likewise, to give them credit, publicly, for their triumphs.

Ike would go on to follow these convictions and give credit to all his subordinates in victory. He was also prepared to take all the blame on D-Day if the invasion had failed. He had even prepared a memo to release if they had experienced failure. The memo that never had to be released said,

> Our landings . . . have failed . . . and I have withdrawn the troops. My decision to attack at this time and place was based upon the

best information available. The troops, the air and the Navy did all that bravery and devotion could do. If any blame or fault attaches to the attempt it is mine alone.

History tells us that Dwight Eisenhower had many personal flaws but was often aware of his shortcomings. What strikes me significantly is that he was a man who was faithfully and humbly carrying out his duties, always seeking to grow and develop. There was nothing glamorous about his life and accomplishments as he entered his 50s. No one expected great things from him, yet Dwight Eisenhower became a five-star general in the United States Army, the Supreme Commander of the Allied Forces in Europe during World War II, and the 34th President of the United States, serving two terms. Clearly, there is power in the humble life.

✦ ✦ ✦

Martin Luther King Jr. was probably the most visible spokesman and leader of the Civil Rights Movement in America. He is best known for advancing civil rights using the tactics of non-violence through civil disobedience.

As you examine his life, it is quite clear that his effectiveness was rooted in humility. In the book, *The 9 Virtues of Exceptional Leaders*, author Rob Jenkins writes of Dr. King's exceptional leadership skills. He refers to the famous "Letter from a Birmingham Jail," where King calls upon white Christian ministers to acknowledge the justice of his cause. This letter has come to be regarded as one of the most significant documents of the Civil Rights Movement. So many of the changes that were championed by Dr. King came to pass rather quickly after this letter was written.

Jenkins asks the question, "What made his arguments so powerful?" It is quite evident that Dr. King approached those he was seeking to influence with great humility. However, it was not from a position of weakness or condescension, or speaking from the moral high ground. He approached them as an equal, as one seeking to be a person of good will who was speaking to another person of good will.

The power of this letter comes in its closing words:

> If I have said anything in this letter that overstates the truth
> and indicates an unreasonable impatience, I beg you to forgive
> me. If I have said anything that understates the truth and indi-
> cates my having a patience that allows me to settle for anything
> less than brotherhood, I beg God to forgive me . . . I hope that
> circumstances will soon make it possible for me to meet each of
> you, not as an integrationist or a civil-rights leader but as . . . a
> Christian brother.

This letter demonstrates how Dr. King was humble and meek, and
yet quite forceful. Though he is challenging the white clergy on their
moral responsibility, in no way does he act condescending toward
them nor come across as if he is morally superior to them.

Two months before he was assassinated, Dr. King delivered his famous sermon about greatness, "The Drum Major Instinct." He made
it quite clear that Jesus gave us a new norm of what it means to be
significant. In his own words, King said,

> If you want to be important—wonderful. If you want to be recog-
> nized—wonderful. If you want to be great—wonderful. But rec-
> ognize that he who is greatest among you shall be your servant.
> That's a new definition of greatness.
>
> And this morning, the thing that I like about it: by giving
> that definition of greatness, it means that everybody can be great,
> because everybody can serve. You don't have to have a college de-
> gree to serve. You don't have to make your subject and verb agree
> to serve. You don't have to know Plato and Aristotle to serve.
> You don't have to know Einstein's theory of relativity to serve.
> You don't have to know the second theory of thermodynamics in
> physics to serve. You only need a heart full of grace, a soul gener-
> ated by love. And you can be that servant.

Rob Jenkins makes this insightful observation about the power of
humility as seen in the life of Dr. Martin Luther King, Jr.:

King's example teaches us something vitally important about humility: Far from the popular conception of "meekness" as a synonym for "weakness," it actually is a form of strength. Or perhaps we should say, rather, that humility is a source of strength, a reservoir of great power.

Leaders who embrace and seek to internalize the virtue of humility do not simply fade into the background, as some might imagine.

IF YOU WANT TO BE GREAT—WONDERFUL. BUT RECOGNIZE THAT HE WHO IS GREATEST AMONG YOU SHALL BE YOUR SERVANT. THAT'S A NEW DEFINITION OF GREATNESS. (MARTIN LUTHER KING, JR.)

They do not become weak and thus prey for the strong in some Darwinian struggle for survival. *Ultimately, they are the fittest, the strongest, and the most capable of leading.*

✦ ✦ ✦

Sam Walker is an editor at *The Wall Street Journal*, and in May 2017 wrote a piece that was adapted from his new book, *The Captain Class: The Hidden Force That Creates the World's Greatest Teams.* In the book, Walker set out to identify the greatest teams in sports history, and to see what each of these teams might have in common. In the end, they all had one shared characteristic. Their years of dominance either began or ended with the tenure of one player. And this player, in every case, eventually became captain of the team.

One of my favorite anecdotes from his book involved the Brazilian soccer team. Back in 1962, when they had won their second consecutive World Cup, Pelé was the star of the team and arguably the greatest soccer player of all time. Most observers assumed that he was the driving force behind the team's success.

However, Pelé was never the captain of the Brazilian soccer team. Behind the scenes was the team's unquestioned leader, Hilderaldo Bellini. Walker describes him as "a tough and humble central defender who during a nine-year stint with Brazil, never scored a goal." Although Bellini was never a star, he performed all the behind-the-scenes tasks necessary to make an exceptional soccer team. Most significantly, he did all the grunt work necessary to unify the team. Bellini recognized that strength is found in unity.

Walker writes, "Bellini cleared up the team's mistakes with his fearless defense, often leaving the pitch bruised and bloodied, and calmly urged them forward when their confidence sagged." He never sought the limelight or desired to be a star.

What is so interesting is the captains of the greatest teams in sports history were not exceptional players. They recognized and accepted their role—not to dazzle on the field of play but to play in the shadows of the stars, to carry the team's water, and to be quite satisfied to lead from the rear. This is humility. There is power in the humble life.

Perhaps one of the most popular people to hold the presidency of the United States was Ronald Reagan. Not only did he have a winsome personality, but he was incredibly humble.

During his eight years in office, one of his great goals was to see the Berlin Wall torn down. He lobbied for it both publicly and also in private conversation with Mikhail Gorbachev. As events spun out of control, in 1989 the people opened the gates, and the following year the official demolition of the Berlin wall began.

What is so interesting is that in 1990, Mikhail Gorbachev, and not Ronald Reagan, was awarded the Nobel Peace Prize. President Reagan, who had fought so hard to see the demolition of the wall, received no credit, yet he never complained. His son Michael wrote these words in his book, *Lessons My Father Taught Me*:

> My father wasn't hungry for praise and applause. He just wanted
> to achieve the goal. One reason my father was willing to let

Mikhail Gorbachev take all the credit was that he knew Gorbachev needed to look like a hero and a leader to his own people, or he would be undermined in his own country. So Dad was willing to give Gorbachev the credit if it would enable Gorbachev to relax the restrictions on the people of East Germany.

Throughout his eight years as president, my father kept a brass plaque on the Resolute desk in the Oval Office that read: "There is no limit to what a man can do or where he can go if he doesn't mind who gets the credit." That was not a mere platitude. That was literally how he lived his life.

Pat Williams points out that the humility of Ronald Reagan is exemplified by his ranch in California where a modest 1,500 square foot Spanish-style ranch house sat on 688 acres. He remodeled it himself after leaving office as governor of California. He hosted many heads of state and prominent visitors in his humble abode. As his son Michael revealed: "My father was a humble man who didn't feel any need to impress other leaders with ostentatious surroundings."

In President Reagan's farewell address to the nation he said,

I never thought it was my style or the words I used that made a difference: it was the content. I wasn't a great communicator, but I communicated great things, and they didn't spring full bloom from my brow, they came from the heart of a great nation—from our experience, our wisdom, and our belief in the principles that have guided us for two centuries . . .

My friends: We did it. We weren't just marking time. We made a difference. We made the city stronger, we made the city freer, and we left her in good hands. All in all, not bad, not bad at all.

What strikes me in these words is that the accomplishments he refers to are described using the plural pronouns "we" and "our." He did not take the credit; he saw it as a joint effort among all of us. This is the mark of a humble leader.

✦ ✦ ✦

C.S. Lewis wrote a wonderful essay entitled, "The Necessity of Chivalry." He points out how in medieval times, the ideal hero was both humble and kind, yet bold and strong. He points to Sir Thomas Mallory's book of the legendary King Arthur and the Knights of the Round Table. In describing Lancelot, Sir Ector says,

> Thou were the meekest man that ever ate in the hall among ladies; and thou were the sternest knight to thy mortal foe that ever put spear in the rest.

Lewis recognized what Jim Collins discovered in his research—strong dynamic people have this paradoxical blend of being humble and kind, yet brave and fearless. Lewis saw that the medieval ideal required this "double demand" from a knight. In the essay he says:

> The knight is a man of blood and iron, a man familiar with the sight of smashed faces and the ragged stumps of lopped-off limbs; he is also a demure, almost a maiden-like, guest in hall, a gentle, modest, unobtrusive man.

STRONG DYNAMIC PEOPLE HAVE THIS PARADOXICAL
BLEND OF BEING HUMBLE AND KIND,
YET BRAVE AND FEARLESS.

Lewis says the chivalrous knight has a duality of character in that he is fierce to the nth degree but is meek and humble as well. He believed that the medieval ideal brought these two qualities together even though they "have no natural tendency to gravitate towards one another."

Lewis is right, most modern people greatly desire to be thought of as strong and courageous. To be considered kind and gentle is of little or no importance, particularly to those in the marketplace.

Lewis recognized that the medieval ideal taught humility and restraint to a valiant knight because everyone knew from experience that he needed it. He realized if it is not possible to produce men who combine the two sides of Lancelot's character, it would not be possible to produce a society with any lasting dignity or happiness.

◆ ◆ ◆

Many people consider Katharine Graham to be one of the most influential women in the 20th century. Born Katharine Meyer in 1917, she was the daughter of Eugene Meyer who bought *The Washington Post* out of bankruptcy in 1933. Katharine began working for the *Post* in 1938 and two years later married Philip Graham, who at the time was working as a clerk for a Supreme Court Justice. Eight years afterward, Meyer made his son-in-law, Philip, the publisher of the *Post*.

As the years went by, Philip struggled with alcoholism and depression. In 1963 he entered a treatment center and eventually was diagnosed as suffering from manic depression. In August 1963, his doctors allowed him to go home for the weekend, where he proceeded to take his life by a self-inflicted shotgun blast.

Katharine was devastated and considered selling the *Post*. However, she finally decided to succeed her husband as publisher. The paper at the time was one of many newspapers in Washington D.C., and none had nearly the readership of the mighty *New York Times*.

Katharine faced her first crisis in 1971 when she made the decision to publish excerpts of the Pentagon Papers, knowing that she and the newspaper staff could be prosecuted under the Espionage Act. She understood that the paper could be financially ruined, but she risked it all for the people's right to know the truth about the Vietnam War. Her decision to print was vindicated on First Amendment, free speech grounds by the Supreme Court.

She showed similar courage when she gave approval to executive editor, Ben Bradlee, and his reporters to pursue the Watergate story. For a long period of time, *The Washington Post* was the only newspaper covering the story, and they received a great deal of pressure and criticism. Once again she was vindicated by her courage to make difficult decisions.

Katharine Graham remained the publisher and head of *The Washington Post* for the next thirty years until her accidental death in 2001. Those who knew her best praised her for two great qualities: courage and humility.

Upon learning of her death, President George W. Bush called her "a true leader and a true lady, steely yet shy, powerful yet humble."

Katharine Graham's funeral service was conducted at Washington National Cathedral. The eulogy was delivered by Senator John Danforth who said this of her:

> Of the many words written this last week, one sentence deserves special attention. It's from Katharine Graham's obituary in the *Post*: "Mrs. Graham was often described as the most powerful woman in the world, a notion she dismissed out of hand.". . . That is an astonishing statement in this town . . .
>
> St. Paul tells us, "Do nothing from selfish ambition or conceit, but in humility regard others as better than yourselves. Let each of you look not to your own interests, but to the interests of others."
>
> That is the way believers are supposed to live . . . It is very biblical and very true that "every one who exalts himself will be humbled, and he who humbles himself will be exalted." That is a text for all of us. It was lived by Katharine Graham.

I read some very interesting words about Mrs. Graham in Pat Williams' book, *Humility*. On his radio program, Pat had interviewed the prominent author and motivational speaker Dr. Sheila Murray Bethel. During the interview, she shared an encounter she had with Katharine Graham back in the late 1990s at a luncheon hosted by Graham. Mrs. Graham's parties and banquets were renowned for their stellar guest lists because she knew so many presidents, kings, and leaders from around the world.

At this particular luncheon, Dr. Bethel was seated next to Mrs. Graham. Bethel asked her,

> Mrs. Graham, you have hosted all the greatest leaders from around the world. What is the single most important trait of all great

leaders? Without hesitation, she said, "The absence of arrogance."

As she reflected back on the conversation, Dr. Bethel says,

> She had stated it so simply, yet it was such a profound insight. As I watched Mrs. Graham conversing with others around the table, it struck me: This woman is the perfect illustration of the trait she named—"absence of arrogance." Katharine Graham was one of the most powerful women in the world—yet it was her humility that defined her. Now, whenever I meet a great leader, I ask myself, "Is this leader humble? Does he or she possess an absence of arrogance?"

In reflecting upon his interview with Dr. Bethel, Williams makes this observation: "I'm here to tell you that the secret ingredient of success, however you define it, in whatever field you seek it, is this trait called humility."

In the February 22, 2014 edition of *The New York Times*, there was a fascinating article by Thomas Friedman entitled, "How to Get a Job at Google." It was written from an interview with Laszlo Bock, the senior vice president in charge of hiring at Google, one of the world's most successful companies.

In the hiring process Bock says, "GPA's are worthless as a criteria for hiring and test scores are worthless; we found they don't predict anything." He then proceeds to share what they are looking for in the prospective new hires that come to interview with Google. One of the primary attributes they desire is humility. They are looking for courageous leaders who, at the appropriate time, will step up and lead but also, at appropriate times, be willing to relinquish power. In other words, they need to be humble enough to step back and embrace the better ideas of others.

Bock also stressed the importance of having intellectual humility for if you do not have this, you will be unable to learn even from failure. Too many proud people believe they are a genius when something good happens; but when something bad happens, it is someone else's fault.

Google seems to understand that truly humble people are what Jim Collins called, "a study in duality: modest and willful, humble and fearless." Bock declares that they are looking for people to take firm positions and who will argue like hell. However, when they learn a new fact, they need to let go of their ego and be willing to change their point of view.

Bock recognizes that in an age of innovation, their work is increasingly a group endeavor. In order to work well and effectively in the group, you have to be humble.

This is in line with something I read in Ryan Holiday's book *Ego is the Enemy*. The nine-time Grammy and Pulitzer Prize winning jazz musician Wynton Marsalis offered this advice to a promising young musician on the mindset required to become a great musician:

> Humility engenders learning because it beats back the arrogance that puts blinders on. It leaves you open for truths to reveal themselves. You don't stand in your own way . . . Do you know how you can tell if someone is truly humble? I believe there's one simple test: because they consistently observe and listen, the humble improve. They don't assume, 'I know the way.'

Holiday says that humble people are students for life and that they seek to learn from everyone and everything. It might be from people you beat or from those who have beaten you. Wherever you are in your life journey, there is the opportunity to learn. This is the perspective humility brings into your life.

~7~

THE MOST HUMBLE PERSON THAT EVER LIVED

IF I WERE TO BOIL DOWN ALL THE
CHARACTERISTICS OF GREATNESS TO A
SINGLE WORD, IT WOULD BE HUMILITY.

—Charles R. Swindoll, pastor and author

~ 7 ~

THE MOST HUMBLE PERSON
THAT EVER LIVED

As we have seen, to be truly humble you have to be kind and gentle but also brave and fearless. You cannot have one without the other. This polarity of characteristics in humility is most clearly seen in the life of Jesus. In Revelations 5:5-6, Jesus is referred to as both a lion and a lamb. In Matthew 11, He refers to Himself as gentle and meek. He is, after all, the God of the universe who has restrained His power to become one of us.

The following words are those of Napoleon at the end of his life, describing the differences between Jesus and himself:

> I die before my time and my body shall be given back to the earth and devoured by worms. What an abysmal gulf between my deep miseries and the eternal Kingdom of Christ. I marvel that whereas the ambitious dreams of myself and of Alexander and of Caesar should have vanished into thin air, a Judean peasant—Jesus—should be able to stretch his hands across the centuries and control the destinies of men and nations.

Here are three famous men—Alexander the Great, Caesar, and Napoleon—seeking to control the world through their own power. When we see their lives contrasted with one man, Jesus, and His humble life as a carpenter, we marvel at how truly extraordinary He must have been that the world was so powerfully changed through His life of humility.

Napoleon goes on to say,

> Time the great destroyer, powerless to extinguish this sacred flame, time can neither exhaust its strength nor put a limit to its range. This is it, which strikes me most. I have often thought of it. This it is which proves to me quite convincingly the divinity of Jesus Christ.

James Stewart, a Scottish philosopher and minister had this to say about the humility of Christ,

> When I speak of the mystery of personality in Christ, I am thinking of the startling coalescence of contrariety that you find in Jesus. He was the meekest and lowliest of all the sons of men, yet He said that he would come on the clouds of heaven in the glory of God. He was so austere that evil spirits and demons cried out in terror at His coming, yet He was so genial, winsome, and approachable that children loved to play with Him, and the little ones nestled in His arms. No one was ever half so kind or compassionate towards sinners, yet no one ever spoke such red hot scorching words about sin. He would not break the bruised reed and His whole life was love, yet on one occasion He demanded of the Pharisees how they expected to escape the damnation of hell. He was a dreamer of dreams and a seer of visions yet for sheer stark naked realism. He has all of our self-styled realists beaten. He was a servant of all, washing the disciples' feet, yet masterfully He strode into the Temple, and the hucksters and traders fell over one another in their mad rush to get away from the fire they saw blazing in His eyes. There is nothing in history to compare with the life of Christ.

Author Henry G. Bosch has made this observation:

> Socrates taught for forty years, Plato for fifty, Aristotle for forty, and Jesus for only three. Yet the influence of Christ's three-year ministry infinitely transcends the impact left by the combined

130 years of teaching from these men who are among the greatest philosophers of all antiquity. Jesus painted no pictures, yet some of the finest paintings of Raphael, Michelangelo, and Leonardo da Vinci received their inspiration from him. Jesus wrote no poetry, but Dante, Milton, and scores of the world's greatest poets were inspired by him. Jesus composed no music, still Haydn, Handel, Beethoven, Bach, and Mendelssohn reached their highest perfection of melody in the hymns, symphonies, and oratorios they composed in his praise. Every sphere of human greatness has been enriched by this humble carpenter of Nazareth.

Use your imagination for a minute. If God gave you the task of creating a life, any life, for your son or your daughter, that would enable them to have a huge influence on the world, what would you choose? Assume you can determine their giftedness, their achievements, their wealth. What would you choose? President of the United States? King of England? Chief Justice of the Supreme Court? Senator? CEO of Apple? A rock star, a movie star, an Academy Award winner, a Heisman trophy winner? What would you choose? Most of us would choose power and influence, some type of celebrity status, a mover and a shaker, or a person of substance whose character, opinions, and actions extended deeply into the world of commerce and politics.

I ask that question because God could have easily provided any of them for Jesus. He could have put him in a wealthy Roman household, or in Athens, where all the scholarly influence resided. God could have given Jesus every advantage you could want in life, but instead He was born and lived in the most desolate part of the Roman Empire called Palestine. He lived a very quiet life with His parents for thirty years as a carpenter. He left almost no traces of Himself on earth, and He never owned any belongings or possessions that could be enshrined in a museum. He never wrote anything. He allowed Himself to be taken into custody. He was mocked, beaten, spat upon, and stripped naked in front of a massive crowd. He was taken to the cross and crucified between two criminals for all the world to see.

This was the ultimate act of humility, that Jesus Himself, the Son of the living God, the King of all Kings, would allow Himself to die a humiliating death on a cross. The Apostle Paul says, "And being found in appearance as a man, He **humbled** Himself by becoming obedient to the point of death, even death on a cross." (Philippians 2:8). And then as hard as it to believe, He asked God the Father to forgive those who executed Him. He was then unceremoniously buried in a borrowed tomb. Yet somehow Jesus and His small following have produced the dominant faith in Western civilization. *How do you explain this?*

Any serious student of history has to scratch his head and wonder how a small band of Christians could survive and even thrive in the ancient Roman world that was bound and determined to eradicate the Christian faith.

World renowned historian Will Durant has written some very interesting words on this topic in his classic book, *The Story of Philosophy*, which is still used in many classrooms as an introduction to philosophy. He is a Pulitzer Prize winning author, but he is most well-known for an eleven-volume series that he and his wife, Ariel, wrote. Although they spent over thirty-five years on this massive work entitled, *The Story of Civilization*, the Durants were not friends of the Christian faith. In this series, one of the volumes covers the history of the Roman Empire; from it we learn that after Jesus' death, the Christian religion was considered to be an enemy of Rome, and this hostility lasted for over 280 years.

In 312 A.D., the edict of Milan went into law legalizing Christianity, specifically Christian worship. In 381 A.D., under Constantine, Christianity became the official religion of the Roman Empire. Durant's observation of what happened in Rome during this period of time is quite astonishing.

There is no greater drama in human record than the sight of a few Christians, scorned and oppressed by a succession of emperors, bearing all trials with a fierce tenacity, multiplying quietly, building order while their enemies generated chaos, fighting the sword with the word, brutality with hope, and at last defeating the strongest state that history has known. Caesar and Christ had met in the arena and Christ had won.

Durant goes on to say,

> That a few simple men should in one generation have invented so powerful and appealing a personality, so lofty an ethic and so inspiring a vision of human brotherhood, would be a miracle far more incredible than any recorded in the Gospels. After two centuries of Higher Criticism, the outlines of the life, character, and teaching of Christ remain reasonably clear and constitute the most fascinating feature in the history of Western man.

TO THE SHOCK AND CONSTERNATION OF HIS FRIENDS
AND SECULAR COLLEAGUES, GIRARD ANNOUNCED
THAT HE HAD BECOME A CHRISTIAN BECAUSE OF THE
UNEXPLAINABLE HUMBLE LIFE OF CHRIST.

Without realizing it, Durant's words are an expression of life's greatest paradox, that strength and power are found in humility.

Philip Yancey wrote in one of his books about the life of French philosopher and anthropologist René Girard, who was a very accomplished individual. He ended his career as a distinguished professor at Stanford. At a certain point in his studies and research, Girard began to notice that a cavalcade of liberation movements had occurred over a relatively short time span—the abolition of slavery, women's suffrage, the Civil Rights movement, women's rights, minority rights, and human rights had gathered speed in the twentieth century. The trend mystified Girard because he found nothing comparable in his readings in ancient literature. Through his further research, Girard traced this phenomenon back to the historical figure of Jesus.

It struck Girard that Jesus' story cuts against the grain of every heroic story from its time. Indeed, Jesus chose poverty and disgrace. He spent his infancy as a refugee. He lived in a minority race under a harsh regime and died as a prisoner. From the very beginning, Jesus took the side of the underdog, the poor, the oppressed, the sick, and the marginalized. His crucifixion, Girard concluded, introduced a new plot to history. *The victim becomes a hero by being a victim.* Girard recognized that two thousand years later, the reverberations of Christ's life have not stopped. Ironically, at the center of the Christian faith hangs a suffering Christ on the cross, dying in shame, for all the world to see.

To the shock and consternation of his friends and secular colleagues, Girard announced that he had become a Christian because of the unexplainable humble life of Christ.

~ 8 ~

THE PATH
TO HUMILITY
PART I

"THANKFULNESS IS A SOIL IN WHICH
PRIDE DOES NOT EASILY GROW."

—*Michael Ramsey, Archbishop of Canterbury*

~ 8 ~

THE PATH TO HUMIILITY,
PART 1

The first place to look as we seek a life of humility is to go back to C.S. Lewis's words in *Mere Christianity*. In the chapter on pride, which he titled "The Great Sin," he closes with these words:

Do not imagine that if you meet a really humble man he will be what most people call "humble" nowadays: he will not be a sort of greasy, smarmy person, who is always telling you that, of course, he is nobody. Probably all you will think about him is that he seemed a cheerful, intelligent chap who took a real interest in what you said to him. If you do dislike him it will be because you feel a little envious of anyone who seems to enjoy life so easily. He will not be thinking about humility: *he will not be thinking about himself at all* (emphasis added).

If anyone would like to acquire humility, I can, I think, tell him the first step. The first step is to realise that one is proud. And a biggish step, too. At least, nothing whatever can be done before it. If you think you are not conceited, it means you are very conceited indeed.

John Dickson says that humble people don't dazzle you with their humility. Even though it is such a powerful force in our lives, it is rather a low-key virtue. I think you may not initially spot a humble person because they are not at all concerned about appearing humble in the eyes of others.

For many of you reading this book, you may have never thought much about pride as it relates to your own life. Most of us are not aware of its presence, yet we so easily see it and despise it when it is clearly present in the lives of others. Yet we all must acknowledge that we battle with the issue of pride, particularly in the thoughts of our hearts. I am reminded of the words of Mary in the Magnificat when she says: "He has done mighty deeds with His arm, He has scattered those who were proud in the thoughts of their heart . . . He has exalted those who were humble" (Luke 1:51, 52).

OUR RESPONSIBILITY

Humility does not come naturally to us. As we grow up, we find that pride is ingrained in our very being as we seek to prove to the world that our lives matter. We want to stand out in the crowd. Very few of us want to be completely out of the limelight with a sense that his or her life is not important.

HUMILITY IS A CHOICE THAT WE MUST
FIRST MAKE AND THEN PURSUE.

One of the most important truths I have learned over the course of my life is that we are responsible for seeking a humble life and cultivating a humble heart. We must therefore realize that humility is a choice that we must first make, and then pursue.

So what are we to do? How does true humility become a reality in our lives? Clearly you cannot flip a switch and become humble or generate humility as an act of your will. It has to be cultivated daily. There is a key phrase in both the Old and New Testaments that gives insight into our responsibility. It is the phrase "humble yourself." We are called to humble ourselves in the presence of God. Consider the following words from the Bible.

> *If My people, who are called by My name humble themselves and pray and seek My face and turn from their wicked ways, then I will hear from heaven, will forgive their sins and will heal their land (2 Chronicles 7:14).*

> *Moses and Aaron went before the Pharaoh and said, "Thus says the Lord, the God of the Hebrews, 'How long will you refuse to humble yourself before Me?'" (Exodus 10:3)*

> *Whoever then humbles himself as this child, he is the greatest in the kingdom of heaven (Mathew 18:4).*

> *Three times it is recorded in the Gospels: "Whoever humbles himself shall be exalted" (Mathew 23:12; Luke 14:11; Luke 18:14).*

> *Humble yourselves in the presence of the Lord, and He will exalt you (James 4:10).*

> *Therefore, humble yourselves under the mighty hand of God, that He may exalt you at the proper time (1 Peter 5:6).*

In his book, *Pride Versus Humility*, Derek Prince says that when God speaks of us humbling ourselves, He is placing this responsibility on us. He says, "We can and we must humble ourselves by a decision of our wills. No one can do this for us—we must do it for ourselves." It clearly is a mandate from God and is our responsibility alone. Prince believes there is a significant principle involved here that was of particular importance to Jesus, and that Christ placed special emphasis on it.

> Jesus continually reminded His hearers that there is a law at work in our lives—one that also governs the entire universe. It is the

law that relates to humility and pride. Here is the way Jesus out-
lines this statute: Whoever exhibits pride will be humbled; whoever exhibits humility will be exalted.

Once more, this precept of which Jesus speaks is universal.
It applies anywhere, to any person, at any time, and in any situation. Often, when I have been teaching on this theme, I have
summed up the precept by saying, "The way up is down; the way
down is up." If we want to go up, we must start by going down;
but if we start by going up, we will end by going down. *Whoever
exalts himself will be humbled, and whoever humbles himself will be
exalted.*"

HUMBLING OURSELVES

We have reached a point now where you are probably wondering,
"What does it mean to humble yourself? How is this done?" The Bible seems to indicate there are a number of ways a person humbles
himself before God. In the balance of this chapter, I am going to lay
out what I believe is the most important way in which we humble
ourselves. However, please know, this is my opinion, and the reason
I believe this is so significant is because it has been so meaningful in
my own life and has changed me.

I want to introduce this thought by walking through some very
instructive verses from the eighth chapter of the book of Deuteronomy. As I go through these verses, I will use some of my own words
to amplify and add commentary to the text.

In the opening verses, God is addressing the Israelites who have
been wandering in the desert for forty years. He then explains what
He has been attempting to accomplish in their lives during this forty-year period of hardship. He says in verse 2 that He did this to
humble them, testing them to know what was in their hearts. In
verse 3, He says that He humbled them by letting them be hungry,
and then feeding them Himself with manna that they did not know
about so that they would understand that human beings do not live

by bread alone. He is telling them life is more than a physical existence, and that we must seek, listen to, and follow God Himself. However, He does not say that over this forty-year period He wanted to teach them to love others or to be morally good. He makes it clear that "I was teaching you to be humble and how to rely on Me."

Then God tells them He is about to lead them into the Promised Land. He describes it in these words:

> For the Lord your God is bringing you into a good land, a land of brooks of water, of fountains and springs, flowing forth in valleys and hills; a land of wheat and barley, of vines and fig trees and pomegranates, a land of olive oil and honey; a land where you shall eat food without scarcity, in which you shall not lack anything; a land whose stones are iron, and out of whose hills you can dig copper (Deuteronomy 8:7-9).

After 40 years of wandering through the desert, He was leading them into what would feel like paradise to them. And in verse 10 He says once they arrive and are experiencing this new life, they are to bless the Lord their God and be thankful for His goodness towards them.

Then God offers them a stern warning. Before He leads them into this wonderful new land and gives them all this prosperity and wonderful surroundings, He warns them, "Beware." Whenever we see God use this word, we should take notice. He warns them about forgetting the Lord their God and not keeping His commandments. Otherwise, what so often happens is that after they have eaten and are fully satisfied and have built beautiful houses and lived in them, and when their herds and flocks multiply, and their silver and gold multiply, and all that they own grows and multiplies, their hearts can become proud and they will forget the Lord their God.

In verse 16, He reminds them again that He fed them manna in the wilderness for forty years to humble them, and He says He did it for their ultimate good and well-being. Then God says something of great significance as it relates to pride and humility. He tells them if they do not remember Him and thank and praise Him, "You will say in your heart, my power and the strength of my hands have made me this wealth." This is the heart of pride and arrogance.

Finally, God provides a key perspective on the humble life in verse 18 when He says, "But you shall remember the Lord your God, for it is He who is giving you the power to make wealth . . ."

Humility begins with understanding who deserves the credit for all that we are and all that we have. When we believe that it comes from ourselves, we will become proud and have no place for God in our lives. However, when we see that all that we are and all that we have is a gift from Him, it will keep us humble; and most significantly, our hearts will naturally overflow with thanksgiving to Him.

At the very end of his life, King David gathered the Jewish assembly together. It was at a time when the nation of Israel was at its very strongest economically, militarily, and spiritually. It would be natural for him to gloat and take at least some of the credit. Instead, you see this prayer of acknowledgment, which are some of the last recorded words of David:

> So, David blessed the Lord in the sight of all the assembly; and David said, "Blessed art Thou, O Lord God of Israel our Father, forever and ever. Thine, O Lord, is the greatness and the power and the glory and the victory and the majesty, indeed everything that is in the heavens and the earth; Thine is the dominion, O Lord, and Thou dost exalt Thyself as head over all. Both riches and honor come from Thee and Thou dost rule over all, and in Thy hand is power and might; and it lies in Thy hand to make great, and to strengthen everyone. Now therefore, our God, we thank Thee, and praise Thy glorious name" (1 Chronicles 29:10).

David recognized who deserved the credit and the glory for the establishment of the great nation of Israel.

This passage reminds me of the words of the famous author Alex Haley who wrote the best-selling novel *Roots*. Haley says that in his office is a picture of a turtle sitting on top of a fence post. He said the picture is there to remind him of a lesson he learned long ago. If you see a turtle on a fence post, he explains, you know he had some help. He says, "Anytime I start thinking, *Wow, isn't this marvelous what*

I have done, look how great I am, I look at that picture and remember how this turtle, me, got up on that post."

We all need to be reminded how we got to where we are today in life.

A HEART OF GRATITUDE

Humble people are grateful people. They recognize who deserves the credit for everything in their lives. True heartfelt thanksgiving is a way in which we humble ourselves. Pride causes us to forget God while thanksgiving causes us to remember Him. Being thankful is a critical issue in our lives because the Bible is replete with the command to "Remember the Lord your God."

The problem is that we are not naturally grateful people. How often do we have to remind our children to say, "Thank you"? If you were to win some type of award, would your first thought be to thank those who helped you along the way and to thank God for your talent, ability, and the opportunities He has given you?

As I have studied the importance of gratitude over the years, I have gained a greater and greater appreciation for its significance and recognize the deadly consequences of ingratitude. Os Guinness says ingratitude is a moral, spiritual, and emotional carelessness about the realities of life. Tim Keller says every time something good happens in your life and you are not grateful to God, you are putting a deep mark on your soul. Author and theologian Warren Wiersbe says, "An ungrateful heart is fertile soil for all types of evil."

I have done a study of the Bible on ingratitude and those who were not thankful and have concluded that ungratefulness is linked to godlessness and evil. The Apostle Paul spells this out clearly in Romans 1:21 when he speaks of people who once knew God but have forgotten Him: "For even though they knew God, they did not honor Him as God or give thanks to Him but their thinking became futile and their foolish hearts were darkened."

Os Guinness says that in the Bible the theme of remembering God is directly linked to giving Him thanks and is inseparable from faith. People of strong faith remember, and those who remember are those who give thanks. Those who forget God are ungrateful. This is true for nations as well as individuals.

The great Nobel Prize winning author Aleksandr Solzhenitsyn made this observation about his own country:

> Over a half century ago, while I was still a child, I recall hearing a number of old people offer the following explanation for the great disasters that had befallen Russia: "Men have forgotten God; that's why all this has happened."
>
> Since then I have spent well-nigh 50 years working on the history of our revolution; in the process I have read hundreds of books, collected hundreds of personal testimonies, and have already contributed eight volumes of my own toward the effort of clearing away the rubble left by that upheaval. But if I were asked today to formulate as concisely as possible the main cause of the ruinous revolution that swallowed up some 60 million of our people, I could not put it more accurately than to repeat: "Men have forgotten God; that's why all this has happened."

BEING INTENTIONALLY GRATEFUL

If you are truly going to cultivate a grateful heart, you are going to have to be intentional about it. It is something you have to plan to do every day. Author Henri Nouwen said,

> In the past I always thought of gratitude as a spontaneous response to the awareness of gifts received, but now I realize that gratitude can also be lived as a discipline. The discipline of gratitude is the explicit effort to acknowledge that all I am and have is given to me as a gift of love, a gift to be celebrated with joy.

Every morning I spend the first ten to fifteen minutes of the day giving thanks to God. I start by acknowledging all that I am and all that I have is a gift from Him and that I am grateful. I thank Him for the gift of life and for a new day. I thank Him for my health and for keeping me in this life (Psalm 66:9). I thank Him for my wife and our life together as well as for our three children. I thank Him for the other relationships He has blessed me with. I thank Him for our home and the financial resources He has provided us. I thank Him for the work He has called me to do and also the talents and abilities he has blessed me with. I give thanks for all the spiritual blessings of life (Ephesians 1:3). Finally, I end by thanking Him for the incredible difference He has made in my life. Where would I be without Him?

I am convinced thanking God has made such a difference in my life. Over time I have found that it leads me to give thanks throughout the day as I recognize His good hand in all that I do. I have come to realize this not only pleases Him, but it has also transformed my life.

This should not be surprising when you consider the research of Dr. Hans Selye, an Austrian-Canadian endocrinologist who died in 1982. Selye was among the first scientists to discover the impact that emotions play on a person's health. Over his life he wrote thirty books on the subject of stress and human emotion. At the end of his life, he summarized his research and concluded that a heart of gratitude is the single most nourishing response that leads to good health. Selye believed that thanksgiving and gratitude are therapy for the soul, and that a healthy soul is beneficial to physical health.

WHAT THE RESEARCH REVEALS

As I was doing research on thanksgiving and gratitude, I discovered two recent articles that presented sound arguments on how gratitude has such a powerful impact on our lives. The first article was from *Psychology Today* and was entitled, "How Gratitude Influences Loving Behavior." The second was from *The Wall Street* Journal and was entitled, "Thanksgiving and Gratitude: The Science of Happier Holidays." The authors of each of these pieces relied on scientific research to come to their conclusions. What we learn from them is:

1. Gratitude is the foundation of satisfying relationships. There is nothing more deadly than when people in a love relationship feel taken for granted.

2. Gratitude expresses appreciation. Human interaction flourishes when people feel appreciated.

3. People who are the most materialistic in our culture are very ungrateful and extremely unhappy. The relationship between materialism and gratitude run in the opposite direction. Ungrateful people are clearly unhappy people.

4. Gratitude acknowledges all the great benefits of life and enables us to savor all that is good in our lives.

5. Finally, and it should come as no surprise, a thankful heart is associated with a number of positive health benefits. Grateful people have stronger immune systems, report fewer symptoms of illness, and enjoy a better quality of sleep. They are also less reactive to stressful events.

Thanksgiving begins with the recognition of who really deserves the credit and glory for what we do. It is most pleasing to God, but it also does something to us. It is life-giving and transformative. Gratitude is where the path of humility begins.

~9~

THE PATH
TO HUMILITY
PART 2

IF YOU PLAN TO BUILD A TALL HOUSE
OF VIRTUES, YOU MUST FIRST LAY DEEP
FOUNDATIONS OF HUMILITY.

—Augustine, theologian and philosopher

~ 9 ~

THE PATH TO HUMIILITY, PART 2

When we humble ourselves, it helps us counter the pride of self-righteousness. Self-righteousness, you will recall, is to believe that you are morally and spiritually superior to others. The self-righteous are convinced their good moral behavior puts them in good standing with God. They come to believe that only good people get into God's kingdom; the bad people, thankfully, are kept out. But this is clearly not the teaching of Christianity. In reality, it is the humble who are let in, and it is the proud and self-righteous who are turned away.

Humility is the lens through which we are able to see God; and as we come to know Him, it enables us to see ourselves as we really are. Jesus communicated this truth in His parable of the Pharisee and the tax collector.

> *Two men went up into the temple to pray, one a Pharisee and the other a tax collector. The Pharisee stood and was praying this to himself: "God, I thank You that I am not like other people: swindlers, unjust, adulterers, or even like this tax collector. I fast twice a week; I pay tithes of all that I get." But the tax collector, standing some distance away, was even unwilling to lift up his eyes to heaven, but was beating his breast, saying, "God, be merciful to me, the sinner!" I tell you, this man went to his house justified rather than the other; for everyone who exalts himself will be humbled, but he who humbles himself will be exalted (Luke 18:9-14).*

The proud Pharisee compares himself to the tax collector when he says, "I thank You I am not like other people . . . even like this tax collector." This Pharisee clearly displays an attitude of moral and spiritual superiority. The tax gatherer, on the other hand, sees only his sin and his need for forgiveness. He is truly humbled by virtue of recognizing his need for forgiveness of his sin.

George Carey, the former Archbishop of Canterbury, made an observation about this parable that provides us with great insight. He describes this very religious, moral Pharisee, who believed in God, as feeling very good about himself. He was comfortable with his standing with God. Yet his pride blinded him, and he did not realize that something was terribly wrong with his life and he was not justified before God. Yet the humble tax gatherer—all the while bowing in his humility and contriteness—was justified before God and forgiven of his sin. At that moment you see a picture of a spiritually healthy and vibrant man—a man who was in right relationship with God.

In this parable Jesus also reveals another way in which we humble ourselves. Here the tax collector with great contrition confesses his sin before God. In reference to his confession Jesus says, "He who humbles himself will be glorified." The parable's meaning is clear—to confess our sins before God is a way we humble ourselves. This is why God tells us in Isaiah 66:2 that the person to whom He looks and has high regard for is the one who is humble, and contrite of spirit, and reveres His Word. There seems to be a clear link between humility and contrition.

Confession of sin is a forgotten practice today. In older traditional church worship services, each service would begin with a general confession of sin. The idea was to get our hearts right as we approach God to worship. You rarely see this happen today in modern worship services.

Many Christians think there is no need for us to confess our sins any longer because a person who puts their faith in Christ has been forgiven of all their sins and has eternal life. There is, therefore, no need to seek God's forgiveness. What they fail to realize is that there are two types of forgiveness.

First, there is what is called "judicial forgiveness." It is the idea of being forgiven or pardoned by a judge who sits in judgment over those who have broken the law. Jesus one day will judge the world. Those who have recognized they are sinful people and have need of God's forgiveness, who recognize that Jesus bore our sins on His body at the cross and then put their faith in Him, will receive judicial forgiveness. They will not have to account for their sins because Jesus accounted for them at the cross. Christ Himself said that these people will not come into judgment (John 5:24) because they are forgiven.

When a person becomes a Christian, they are adopted into God's family, and He becomes their heavenly Father and is no longer their judge. As a child of God, they now have a new relationship with Him. So when Christians sin, it affects our relationship with our heavenly Father. Therefore we confess our sins to Him for the good of the relationship. Sin causes separation between us and God, and it keeps us from being close to Him. His forgiveness brings us together and re-connects us. This is what is called "fatherly forgiveness." We must confess our sin daily in order to have a close, growing relationship with our heavenly Father.

TO CONFESS OUR SINS BEFORE GOD IS
A WAY WE HUMBLE OURSELVES.

The book of James gives some insight into the relationship between humility, humbling ourselves, and confession of sin. In James 4:6 we are told God is opposed to the proud but gives grace to the humble. In verse eight, we are told to draw near to God and He will draw near to us. He says that before we can draw near, as sinners we must cleanse our hands and our hearts. We need to cleanse ourselves from not only the outer sins that people see but also the inner sins of the heart. As one commentator put it, "Your hands and heart symbolize your deeds and thoughts." Therefore, in order to really draw near to God, we must cleanse ourselves, and this is done by the confession of sin. Confessing our sin is, as Jesus said, a way we humble ourselves before God.

DEPENDING ON GOD

In the work that I do with businessmen, one truth that is quite apparent to me is that we all have struggles of some kind. We all are fighting some type of battle, sometimes on multiple fronts. However, we feel compelled not to show any weakness because as leaders we are not supposed to struggle; we are supposed to be competent and always have our act together.

As I said earlier, spiritual pride is the belief that we do not need God. Yet to truly humble ourselves, we have to be willing to acknowledge that we are weak and needy and not masters of the universe.

Theologian Ole Hallesby said, "The word 'helplessness' is the single best word to describe the heart attitude we bring before God." This principle is very difficult for modern people who have been taught all their lives to be self-reliant and self-sufficient. If we are not careful, we can seal off the heart attitude that is most desirable to God. Philip Yancey says that the heart of prayer is a declaration of our dependence upon God.

John Calvin believed a major component of the humble life was seeing our weaknesses and inadequacy, which then generates a strong sense of our need to depend on God. He believed we needed to be ruthlessly honest about our flaws, our weaknesses, and our struggles before God, recognizing our hope for inner strength and power comes from God alone.

King David was a great and mighty warrior and king. Yet when you read his words and prayers in the Psalms, you see a man who was utterly dependent upon God. He openly shares his deficiencies, his fears, and his sin. His prayers declare his great needs. One of his prayers that I love to pray myself is Psalm 30:10, "Hear, O Lord and be gracious to me; O Lord, be my helper."

We humble ourselves when we go before God, declare our great needs before Him, and attest that He is our ultimate hope and adequacy. The Apostle Paul offers some interesting insight. In 2 Corinthians 12, Paul speaks of a thorn in his flesh that was given to him. We do not know what this thorn actually was, but it was quite troubling to him. He tells us the purpose of this thorn was to keep him from exalting himself. Like all of us, Paul clearly struggled with pride. He then goes on to say,

> *"Three times I pleaded with the Lord to take it away from me. But He said to me, 'My grace is sufficient for you, for my power is made perfect in weakness.' Therefore I will boast all the more gladly about my weaknesses, so that Christ's power may rest on me. That is why, for Christ's sake, I delight in weaknesses, in insults, in hardships, in persecutions, in difficulties. For when I am weak, then I am strong"* (2 Corinthians 12:8-10).

God made it clear that He was not going to remove this thorn, but would instead give Paul the strength and power (His grace) to turn this weakness into a strength. Moreover, God desires to give all of us His grace to help us in our weaknesses. Paul says that when we acknowledge our weaknesses before God, we find His strength. "When I am weak, then I am strong."

We humble ourselves before God when we acknowledge, "Lord I need You; I need Your strength. I cannot deliver myself from pride, greed, anger, and from judging others. I look to You to enable me to do that which I cannot do myself."

Life's greatest paradox is that strength is found in humility.

KEEPING A SECRET

A fourth way we humble ourselves can be very helpful in keeping us from seeking to impress others. Have you ever thought how much our lives are focused on what John Ortberg calls "impression management." So much of what we say and do is intended to impress others. We may casually name drop, mention our child's accomplishments, or talk about an exotic place where we have vacationed in the past. This happened even back in New Testament times, as Jesus says of the Pharisees, "They do all of their deeds to be noticed by men" (Matthew 23:5).

Sociologist George Herbert Mead explains this principle in a concept called "the generalized other." In our minds, there are certain people on whose judgment we measure our success and failure. Our lives are validated by what they think of us. However, the problem is that we never know in totality what any one person actually thinks of us.

Jesus provides some great instruction on this issue. He says,

> Beware of practicing your righteousness before men to be noticed by them; otherwise you have no reward with your Father who is in heaven. So when you give to the poor, do not sound a trumpet before you, as the hypocrites do in the synagogues and in the streets, so that they may be honored by men. Truly I say to you, they have their reward in full. But when you give to the poor, do not let your left hand know what your right hand is doing, so that your giving will be in secret; and your Father who sees what is done in secret will reward you (Matthew 6:1-4).

The philosopher Dallas Willard has written some thoughts on what he calls "the discipline of secrecy." He says that we should intentionally abstain from seeking to make our good deeds and qualities known, although it should never involve deceit. He believes we should look to God to enable us to tame our hunger for fame and trying to gain the attention of others. Over time, as we practice this discipline, we will learn to embrace anonymity without the loss of our peace, joy, or purpose.

Willard says one of the great tragedies in our lives is holding the belief that all our virtues and accomplishments need to be advertised. We have this deep yearning that they must be known. The discipline of secrecy, rightly practiced, enables us to place all our public relations in the hands of God. By doing this, we allow Him to decide when our deeds need to be known. Willard says, "When we desire godly secrecy, our love and humility before God will develop to the point we'll not only see our friends, family, and associates in a better light, but we'll also develop the virtue of desiring their good above our own."

Back in the 1930s and 1940s, the most popular English novelist was a man by the name of Lloyd C. Douglas. He began his adult life as a Christian pastor and then became a writer.

Five of his books were made into movies. One of the most popular, *The Robe*, was made into a movie, which starred Richard Burton. It won two academy awards and was nominated for best picture. He also wrote an incredibly popular novel in 1929 entitled *Magnificent Obsession* which was made into a movie, twice. I had the opportunity to read this novel three or four years ago, and it was a fascinating book. (I read that this was one of John Wooden's favorite novels.)

The story is about Dr. Wayne Hudson who is struggling with deep depression and is on the edge of failure in his work. His wife has just died, and he goes to purchase a marker for her grave. As he looks at the various monuments, he encounters an eccentric but very talented sculptor by the name of Clive Randolph. They begin to engage in a conversation, and over time as they become more comfortable with each other, Randolph imparts to him a secret that he claims will transform the doctor's life.

Though Randolph does not completely lay out this wonderful secret all at once, when you piece it together it goes like this: Most people live depleted lives; they are weak, zestless, and have very little energy. The reason, he contends, is that when we perform a good deed or some worthy achievement we want the world to know about it. We seek to advertise it and receive all the credit for it. On the other hand, when our lives are not going well and we are floundering, we carefully hide our problems or look for ways to deny them if we can. Randolph says that people, therefore, spend their lives pretending, always insecure and afraid of being found out.

Randolph tells Dr. Hudson that to remedy this situation and find power in his life, the simple secret is to reverse the strategy. In other words, he needed to keep his great deeds and accomplishments a secret and find people with whom he was willing to be vulnerable and share with them his struggles, fears, and secrets. Dr. Hudson began to apply this in his own life, and his depression lifted and he later became a famous brain surgeon.

Dr. Hobart Mowrer was a famous American psychologist who was fascinated by this novel, particularly with Randolph's secret formula. Dr. Mowrer decided to conduct some research into the life of Lloyd C. Douglas. He spent time interviewing Douglas's daughter, seeking to determine if her father had actually practiced Clive Randolph's secret formula for power.

Mowrer said it was not surprising "that until he was 50 years old, Douglas was a good but not outstanding minister and then, suddenly, became and remained to the end of his life the most widely read novelist in the English language." Mowrer concluded that if all the facts were known, Lloyd C. Douglas's own life would dramatically testify to the power of this principle which he called "the magnificent obsession."

DIFFICULT TO DETECT

In the opening chapter we looked at the words of C.S. Lewis and he said that one of the real problems with pride is how difficult it is to detect its presence in our own lives. We easily see it in the lives of others but are often blind to our own pride and arrogance.

Jesus gives us a glimpse into this problem in the Sermon on the Mount in Matthew 7:3, when He asks, "Why do you look at the speck that is in your brother's eye, but do not notice the log in your own eye?" He tells us that we need to focus on and deal with the logs in our own eye.

I have concluded that if we are to become humble people, we need to be aware of our pride and those moments when it is about to rear its ugly head. I regularly pray and ask God to show me the logs in my life, particularly the pride in my heart. However, let me warn you that God is faithful, and He will begin to show you your pride, and sometimes it can be really ugly when you see your heart. However, it will strip you of your self-righteousness and humble you when you clearly see the depravity of your own heart. I would encourage you to pray this daily as you seek to cultivate a humble heart.

~ 10 ~

PRIDE, HUMILITY AND FAITH

"THE POINT OF THE DEATH OF CHRIST IS
THAT CHRIST TOOK ON THE SINS OF THE
WORLD, SO THAT WHAT WE PUT OUT
DID NOT COME BACK TO US, AND THAT
OUR SINFUL NATURE DOES NOT REAP
THE OBVIOUS DEATH. THAT'S THE POINT.
IT SHOULD KEEP US HUMBLED... IT'S NOT
OUR OWN GOOD WORKS THAT GET US
THROUGH THE GATES OF HEAVEN."

–Bono, lead singer U2

~ 10 ~

PRIDE, HUMILITY
AND FAITH

C.S. Lewis says that it is the pride of life that keeps us from knowing God. As he looked back upon his own life, he recognized that his great desire to be famous (pride) had been a major stumbling block in his coming to a life of faith. I also see this in the lives of so many men with whom I meet. On the other hand, it is humility that provides the eyes that allow us to see God.

If you will remember back in Chapter five I said that pride causes us to be independent from God. We think we can run our lives just fine without Him and achieve all our goals and prosperity on our own. Our prideful hearts cause us to believe that "I don't need God."

In these last two chapters, we will consider the relationship between humility and faith. This is the heart of Christianity, and it will determine how we relate to God and whether we will ever personally know Him.

PRIDE AND FAITH

A number of years ago I met with a man who was on a search for spiritual truth. We met several times and discussed a number of issues; in our last meeting, I very slowly and deliberately explained the Gospel message to him. He told me that he believed what I had told him was true. However, he made it clear that he did not want to be a Christian.

As I look back on that encounter, his reasoning was quite revealing. He explained to me that becoming a true follower of Christ
would harm him socially and in his career. He was convinced that
many of his friends would reject him and that he might be frowned
upon in the business world. In the end, he rejected the truth of God
because he feared what people would think of him. This is what pride
will do to you, and I have seen it play out many times in people's life.

Blaise Pascal noticed a pattern in many of his intellectual friends.
They had no interest in spiritual truth because they feared the opinions of their friends, and dreaded being labeled weak and religious.
Pascal saw clearly how much they desired to court the favor of
worldly, successful people. He saw right through them, recognizing
that they were always posturing to create an image that they were
strong and confident. He found it hard to believe that any sensible
person would show no interest in the ultimate issues of life out of
fear of what people would think of them. This is another example of
pride being an obstacle to faith.

An author I have really grown to admire is Dr. Paul Vitz, a retired
psychologist who taught at New York University. Vitz was an atheist
until his mid-thirties, and in his book *A Place for Truth*, he shares
some interesting insight on why he originally rejected God. He says,

> The major reason for me wanting to become an atheist was that
> I desired to be accepted by the powerful and influential psychol-
> ogists in my field. In particular I wanted to be accepted by my
> professors in graduate school. As a graduate student I was thor-
> oughly socialized by the specific culture of academic psychology.
> My professors at Stanford, as much as they might disagree on
> psychological theory, were, as far as I could tell, united on really
> only two things: their intense personal ambition and their rejec-
> tion of religion . . .
>
> In this environment, just as I had learned how to dress like a
> college student by putting on the right clothes, I also learned to
> "think" like a proper psychologist by putting on the right—that
> is, atheistic—ideas and attitudes.

Do you hear what Dr. Vitz is saying? He desperately wanted to be accepted by his peers and professors. He is saying, "I feared their rejection and yearned for their approval so much so that I adopted their views, whether I believed them to be true or not." He reveals that this was the audience he was seeking to please. In effect, he allowed their opinions to set the boundaries of his own faith and beliefs. Pride is a huge obstacle to faith.

One of the great miracles in the Bible is in the book of John, when Jesus raises His friend Lazarus who had been dead for four days. If you read John chapters 11 and 12, you will recognize what an eruption it caused among the Jews and religious leaders. In John 12:42, it says even some of the Jewish leaders believed but did not profess their belief openly for fear of being put out of the synagogue. However, in verse 43 you see the real reason. The text says ". . . for they loved the approval of man more than they loved the approval of God." What we do not realize is how our pride causes us to arrange our lives to meet the expectations and approval of others.

> WHAT WE DO NOT REALIZE IS HOW OUR PRIDE CAUSES US TO ARRANGE OUR LIVES TO MEET THE EXPECTATIONS OF OTHERS.

Priest and psychotherapist Anthony de Mello provides a powerful analysis of our prideful condition:

Look at your life and see how you have filled its emptiness with people. As a result they have a stranglehold on you. See how they control your behavior by their approval and disapproval. They hold the power to ease your loneliness with their company, to send your spirits soaring with their praise, to bring you down to the depths with their criticism and rejection. Take a look at yourself spending almost every waking moment of your day placating and pleasing people, whether they are living or dead. You live by their norms, conform to their standards, seek their company, desire their love, dread their ridicule, long for their applause, meekly submit to the guilt they lay upon you; you are terrified to go against the fashion in the way you dress or speak or act or even think.

Pride makes us weak and causes us to be duplicitous. It is hard to believe that we will allow other people's opinions of us determine the way we see ourselves and how we make decisions on issues with grave consequences.

When it gets right down to it, whose opinion of our lives counts the most? When you get to the end of your life, whose opinion will matter most? The answer to this question will ultimately determine whether pride or humility will rule in your heart.

WHO IS MY AUDIENCE?

Andrew Carnegie was a Scottish-American industrialist who led the expansion of the steel industry in America in the late 19th century. He is often identified as one of the wealthiest Americans who ever lived.

Carnegie was born in Dunfermline, Scotland, but grew up in Pittsburgh. When he was a young boy, he found his mother one day weeping in despair. Young Andrew tried to console her and urged her not to cry. He confidently assured her that one day he would be wealthy and that they would ride in a fine coach pulled by four fine horses. His mother replied, "That will do no good over here if no one in Dunfermline can see us."

Andrew Carnegie made up his mind that day that he and his mother would one day make a grand entry into Dunfermline in a royal coach drawn by the finest horses so that the entire town could witness the event. He would show them. Making it big in Pittsburgh was not enough. He had to prove the family's success in front of their hometown audience.

A little over thirty years later, Andrew and his mother returned to Scotland. He had become one of the world's richest men. The trip had been long planned with his mother and a select group of their friends. There was an official parade with the climax of the day being Carnegie's bestowal of the funds for a new, beautiful library on the city of his birth. For he and his mother, this was a magnificent day of triumph. They both had longed to win the approval of an audience that they valued so much—the people of Dunfermline. Andrew Carnegie and his mother had shown them. Despite the initial success of the library, it was soon found to be too small and the layout unsuitable. Their initial prideful bequest turned sour.

Os Guinness, in his book, *The Call*, uses this story to help us understand the audience for whom we seek to perform. Have you ever thought about that? Guinness says,

> Most of us, whether we are aware of it or not, do things with an
> eye to the approval of some audience or other. The question is not
> *whether* we have an audience but *which* audience we have.

Here again you see how pride rears its ugly head in our lives. It is one thing to have certain aims and ambitions, but we somehow have come to believe that any of our achievements or accomplishments are worthless unless the audience we value the most knows about it. Most people live their entire lives looking for ways to win the approval of their audience because it makes them feel like their lives are worthwhile and have significance.

The problem is, we have gotten this all wrong. Several years ago, popular author Donald Miller gave a lecture to a large group of students at Harvard, and he addressed this issue. This is what he said:

> Human beings are wired so that they need some great authority
> outside themselves to tell him or her who they really are. But for
> many people that voice is not there, because their lives are not
> oriented towards God. When that is the case, the very first thing
> that will happen in their lives will be to question their worth and
> their value. Does my life really matter? And this is what causes us
> to begin to hide ourselves from others.

WE WERE DESIGNED TO LIVE SO THAT THE AUDIENCE
WE SEEK TO PLEASE FIRST IS GOD.

Miller goes on to say that he recognizes this to be true in the lives of everyone, including important people and famous celebrities. When he realized how we no longer look to God to give us our worth and significance, he understood why we are so addicted to the approval of others, particularly the audience we are trying to impress.

The problem is we are seeking to impress the wrong audience! We were designed to live so that the audience we seek to please first is God. Os Guinness puts it this way, "A life lived listening to the decisive call of God is a life lived before one audience that trumps all others—the Audience of One."

This is where humility begins. Getting this right changes everything.

THE LOOKING GLASS SELF

One of the best ways to understand this is to consider Charles Cooley's landmark theory called the "looking glass self." Cooley was a prominent sociologist who lived from 1864 to 1929. The "looking glass self" is a human development theory that is timeless in its application to our lives. In its simplest form, the theory states:

> A person gets his identity in life based on how the most important person in his life sees him.

For a young child, of course, it is the parent. We all know how important it is for parents to encourage and build up their children because we have such an impact on their sense of worth as they develop. However, as the child grows and becomes a teenager, the parents inevitably discover they are no longer their child's number one audience. Most parents, for better or for worse, have been almost completely replaced by their child's peer group. Most teenagers value their peers' opinions more than anything else, and most parents realize that peer pressure is a very powerful force in the lives of their teenage children.

For an adult, particularly an adult out in the workplace, the opinion valued the most will typically come from a colleague or peer. We greatly value what other men and women in the workplace and in the community think of us. They are our audience, and we perform for them. We yearn to hear their praise.

And, sadly, whether as a teenager or as an adult, we often unconsciously allow our audience to make the final verdict on the value of our lives. The reality, however, is that the verdict is not in because our performance is never over. No matter how much applause we received yesterday, we can't be certain we will receive it again tomorrow.

What do you think would happen to people if Jesus Christ became the most important person in their lives? What if Christ was the audience they sought to please most? How would it change them? I contend it would change them radically because Christ does not love and accept us based on our performance. He loves us because we are of such great value to Him.

C.S. Lewis truly understood his identity and who his true audience was. Armand Nicholi tells us that after Lewis became a Christian, he read the Bible voraciously, and it began to transform him. Nicholi shares:

> As Lewis began to read the Old and New Testaments seriously, he noted a new method of establishing his identity, of coming to terms with his "real personality." This process, Lewis writes, involves losing yourself in your relationship to the Creator. "Until you have given yourself up to Him," Lewis writes, "you will not have a real self."

Therein lies the solution to finding our true identity as people. What Lewis recognized is that if you are really going to find your life and

live it to the fullest, you have to give up your life and surrender it to
Christ. This surrender is the ultimate act of humility.

...IF YOU ARE REALLY GOING TO FIND YOUR LIFE AND
LIVE IT TO THE FULLEST, YOU HAVE TO GIVE UP YOUR
LIFE AND SURRENDER IT TO CHRIST. THIS SURRENDER IS
THE ULTIMATE ACT OF HUMILITY.

A PICTURE OF PRIDE AND HUMILITY

Probably the most well-known of all of Jesus' parables is found in
Luke 15:11-32. It is known as the parable of the Prodigal Son, but in
reality it is a parable about a loving father (who represents God) and
two sons who represent the human race. In this simple story, you
see how pride, humility, and coming to faith intersect. I will walk
through the parable, making comments along the way.

A man had two sons and the younger son approached him and
asked for the share of the estate that would one day be due him. Surprisingly, the father said yes. A few days later, the young son gathered
all his wealth and possessions and traveled to a distant country. He
then proceeded to squander his wealth on reckless and wild living.

This young son left his home looking for a better life, and he seemed
to think he knew where to find it. He left with a real sense of freedom.
I am sure he had the same attitude so many young people have today—
they are bullet-proof and are going out to conquer the world.

Most significantly, he wanted to get away from his father's presence. The young son wanted his father's money and financial support
but did not really want anything to do with his father. This is so true
of us. We want the blessings of God—we just don't want God in our
lives.

Spiritual pride is clearly present in the life of the young son. It is
as if he wanted to prove to the world that he did not need his father
and his father's love and, in essence, said, "I can make it on my own. I

want to be fully independent and autonomous." Furthermore, he did not want to live under his father's authority; he wanted the freedom to live however he chose to live.

Unfortunately, this is the way we are with God. We arrogantly think we do not need Him and can live just fine without Him. We overlook the fact that we are weak, sinful human beings, and living in humble reliance upon Him is how we were designed to function best. It is too easy for us to see God's will as nothing more than a bunch of rules He has given us to regulate our lives. In reality, all of God's teaching and instruction is like an owner's manual for our lives, pointing to God's deliberate design for human life. When we follow the owner's manual, our lives flourish.

As the parable continues, the young son squandered everything he had and ended up with a job feeding pigs. No one was giving him anything. He was truly humbled, and I am sure he realized that he was not, in fact, bullet-proof. His pursuit of the good life had broken down; and because his money was gone, no one around him seemed to really care.

The young son's arrogance blinded him to the realities of life. This is what pride does. Being humbled by his circumstances gave him the eyes to see. We are told in the text that he "came to his senses." He recognized how lost he was. I am sure he finally realized the cold hard fact that the world was not devoted to his happiness or well-being. He also recognized his true condition—he was dead and lost. This is the condition we find ourselves in when we are not walking in faith. Our pride causes us to think we know everything; we have life figured out. This is what this young son believed until he came to his senses.

The parable goes on to say that the son finally recognized his need for his father. He was now able to see clearly and realized there was someone who loved him and cared for his life. He knew his father at least would give him a job. However, in order to return to his father, he saw the need to do two essential things.

First, he recognized that he was a sinner and needed to confess his sins. The text says, "I will get up and go to my father, and will say to him 'Father, I have sinned against heaven and in your sight; I am no longer worthy to be called your son.'" The son recognized his need for his father's forgiveness. As you will recall, asking for forgiveness is a way we humble ourselves before God.

The second realization the son comes to, is that in order to get back into right relationship with his father, he has to leave his wayward lifestyle and return home on his father's terms. He could not go back on his own terms. The son was leaving his old life for a new life.

This is what happens in the lives of so many people. They want to be a Christian but only on their own terms. A true believer is one who is willing to surrender their will to Christ and follow Him. It means turning our heart away from self and turning toward God. This surrender is at the core of repentance, and it requires us to humble ourselves before God.

C.S. Lewis says that what made atheism so attractive to him was that he could gratify his wishes and live however he pleased. This was true of the young son in the parable. However, when Lewis came to believe in God, and then recognized that Jesus was the Son of God who had died for his sins on the cross, it was only logical for him to surrender. It is like choosing to serve in the army of a powerful king. You do not negotiate with the king and tell him what you are willing to do. You bend your knee to him and serve him with your life.

Lewis says this in his book, *Mere Christianity*,

Now what was the sort of "hole" man had got himself into? He had tried to set up on his own, to behave as if he belonged to himself. In other words, fallen man is not simply an imperfect creature who needs improvement: he is a rebel who must lay down his arms. Laying down your arms, surrendering, saying you are sorry, realizing that you have been on the wrong track and getting ready to start life over again from the ground floor—that is the only way out of our "hole." This process of surrender—this movement full speed astern is what Christians call repentance.

Lewis is saying that the arrogance of man insists, "I belong to myself and I will run the show." The Christian humbles himself and declares, "I surrender and I will follow you."

THE HOMECOMING

So the son returned home and was shocked at what awaited him.

> And he got up and came to his father. But while he was still a long way off, his father saw him, and felt compassion for him, and ran and embraced him, and kissed him.
>
> And the son said to him, "Father, I have sinned against heaven and in your sight; I am no longer worthy to be called your son."
>
> But the father said to his slaves, "Quickly bring out the best robe and put it on him, and put a ring on his hand and sandals on his feet; and bring the fattened calf, kill it, and let us eat and be merry; for this son of mine was dead, and has come to life again; he was lost, and has been found." And they began to be merry.

As we examine the response of the father, we need to remember that it was he who let the son go his own way. God designed us to live in His presence, to know Him, to live under his authority and follow His plan for our lives—it is the concept of following the owner's manual, knowing it leads to our ultimate well-being. However, God will allow us to leave His presence, go to the distant land, and live however we choose. He will even allow us to self-destruct. However, He is always waiting for us to humble ourselves and return.

The parable ends with the older brother, who was faithfully working out in the field, hearing all the commotion of the party. He summoned one of the servants and asked what was going on. The servant told him, "Your brother has come home, and your father has killed the fatted calf because he has received him back safe and sound."

As you might imagine, the older son became angry and refused to join in the celebration. The father went out to plead with him, but he refused. The father's last words in the parable are: "We had to celebrate and be glad, because this brother of yours was dead and is alive again, he was lost and is found."

The older son suffered from pride as well—the pride of self-righteousness. He was very judgmental and experienced a joyless obedience. He had no compassion for his younger brother, and he did not understand the father's forgiveness. How could he ever forgive him?

Henry Nouwen in his wonderful book, *The Return of the Prodigal Son*, lays out a wonderful contrast of the waywardness of the two brothers. He says,

> Often we think about lostness in terms of actions that are quite visible, even spectacular. The younger son sinned in a way we can easily identify. His lostness is quite obvious. He misused his money, his time, his friends, his own body. What he did was wrong; not only his family and friends knew it, but he himself as well. He rebelled against morality and allowed himself to be swept away by his own lust and greed. There is something very clear-cut about his misbehavior. Then, having seen that all his wayward behavior led to nothing but misery, the younger son came to his senses, turned around, and asked for forgiveness. We have here a classical human failure, with a straightforward resolution. Quite easy to understand and sympathize with.
>
> The lostness of the elder son, however, is much harder to identify. After all, he did all the right things. He was obedient, dutiful, law-abiding, and hardworking. People respected him, admired him, praised him, and likely considered him a model son. Outwardly, the elder son was faultless. But when confronted by his father's joy at the return of his younger brother, a dark power erupts in him and boils to the surface. Suddenly, there becomes glaringly visible a resentful, proud, unkind, selfish person, one that had remained deeply hidden, even though it had been growing stronger and more powerful over the years.

In this story, the celebration that is thrown is representative of heaven. And though it is just a parable, in the end the younger brother went into the celebration, and the older brother did not. The younger son has humbled himself, the older brother has not.

Tim Keller says that people who say, "I am a Christian, look at all my good works and accomplishments" do not realize they are spiritually lost. God is going to say to them, "But I never knew you . . .You don't know what the cross of Jesus means" (Matthew 7:21-23).

On the other hand, those who come and say, "Lord, I am a sinner; I repent; I need your grace; I have nothing to merit your favor" and pray for salvation in Jesus' name, will find salvation. This is what it means to be saved by grace through faith.

Keller says that is a picture of humility. He says that to not approach God with humility and contriteness can lead to eternal destruction. Humility is what connects you to God because God's plan of salvation is to lift up the humble.

~ I I ~

HOW A
PRIDEFUL MAN FINDS
HIS FAITH

"FOR THE LORD TAKES PLEASURE IN HIS
PEOPLE: HE ADORNS THE HUMBLE
WITH SALVATION.

—Psalm 149:4

~ 11 ~

HOW A PRIDEFUL MAN
FINDS HIS FAITH

A person whose books have had a profound impact on my life
is Charles "Chuck" Colson. His life story is quite fascinating.
Colson was born in Boston on October 16, 1931. He was
well educated, graduating with honors from Brown University with
a degree in history. He went on to George Washington University
where he received his law degree. He then spent two years in the
U.S. Marine Corps where he reached the rank of captain. From there
he founded his own law firm in Boston, which swiftly grew into a
prestigious organization with offices in Boston and Washington
D.C. Colson left the firm in January 1969 to join Richard Nixon's
administration in the White House. In November of that same year,
he was appointed as Special Counsel to the president.

Colson acknowledged in his own words, "I was valuable to the
president, because I was willing to be ruthless in getting things
done." He was described by many as President Nixon's "hit man" and
"hatchet man." He was a very hard, vindictive person and very loyal
to President Nixon.

At the height of the Watergate scandal, Colson gained notori-
ety for being named as one of the Watergate Seven and eventually
pleaded guilty to obstruction of justice. He was charged with attempting to defame Pentagon Papers defendant Daniel Ellsberg.

Colson shares an event that happened while he was facing time
in prison that forever changed his life. He had a good friend by the
name of Tom Phillips who was president of Raytheon, a Fortune 500
company and the largest firm in Massachusetts at the time. One day,

Colson was told that something had happened to Tom. He heard that Phillips had some kind of religious experience, and that he had changed quite a bit. Apparently, his new-found faith had become quite important to him.

The Watergate hearings were really beginning to heat up, and so Colson and his wife decided to get away and drive up to the Maine coast. Since they would be driving through Boston, he decided to stop by and visit Tom.

The following are excerpts from that evening as described by Colson himself from his memoir *Born Again*:

It was eight p.m., a gray overcast evening, when I turned off the country road connecting two of Boston's most affluent suburbs, Wellesley and Weston. The towering gentle pines brought sudden darkness and quiet to the narrow macadam street. Another turn a few hundred yards later brought me into a long driveway leading to the Phillipses' big white clapboard Colonial home. As I parked the car I felt a touch of guilt at not telling Patty the truth when I had left her alone with my mother and dad in nearby Dover.

"Just business, honey," had been my explanation. Patty was used to my working at odd times, even on this Sunday night at the start of a week's vacation.

The Phillipses' home is long and rambling. I made the mistake of going to the door nearest the driveway, which turned out to be the entrance to the kitchen. It didn't bother Gert Phillips, a tall smiling woman who greeted me like a long-lost relative even though we had never met before. "Come in. I'm just cleaning up after supper."

After exchanging pleasantries with the Phillips family, Tom and Chuck walked to a screened-in porch at the end of the house.

"Tell me, Chuck," he began, "are you okay?"

As the President's confidant and so-called big-shot Washington lawyer I was still keeping my guard up. "I'm not doing too badly, I guess. All of this Watergate business, all the accusations – I suppose it's wearing me down some. But I'd rather talk about you, Tom. You've changed and I'd like to know what happened."

Tom drank from his glass and sat back reflectively. Briefly he reviewed his past, the rapid rise to power at Raytheon: executive vice-president at 37, president when he was only 40. He had done it with hard work, day and night, nonstop.

"The success came, all right, but something was missing," he mused. "I felt a terrible emptiness. Sometimes I would get up in the middle of the night and pace the floor of my bedroom or stare out into the darkness for hours at a time."

"I don't understand it," I interrupted. "I knew you in those days, Tom. You were a straight arrow, good family life, successful, everything in fact going your way."

"All that may be true, Chuck, but my life wasn't complete. I would go to the office each day and do my job, striving all the time to make the company succeed, but there was a big hole in my life. I began to read the Scriptures, looking for answers. Something made me realize I needed a personal relationship with God, [it] forced me to search."

A prickly feeling ran down my spine. Maybe what I had gone through in the past several months wasn't so unusual after all—except I had not sought spiritual answers. I had not even been aware that finding a personal relationship with God was possible. I pressed him to explain the apparent contradiction between the emptiness inside while seeming to enjoy the affluent life.

"It may be hard to understand," Tom chuckled. "But I didn't seem to have anything that mattered. It was all on the surface. All the material things in life are meaningless if a man hasn't discovered what's underneath them."

We were both silent for a while as I groped for understanding. Outside, the first fireflies punctuated the mauve dusk. Tom got up and switched on two small lamps on end tables in the corners of the porch.

"One night I was in New York on business and noticed that Billy Graham was having a Crusade in Madison Square Garden," Tom continued. "I went—curious, I guess—hoping maybe I'd find some answers. What Graham said that night put it all into place for me. I saw what was missing, the personal relationship with

Jesus Christ, the fact that I hadn't ever asked Him into my life, hadn't turned my life over to Him. So I did it—that very night at the Crusade."

Tom's tall, gangling frame leaned toward me, silhouetted by the yellow light behind him. Though his face was shaded, I could see his eyes begin to glisten and his voice became softer. "I asked Christ to come into my life and I could feel His presence with me, His peace within me. I could sense His spirit there with me. Then I went out for a walk alone on the streets of New York. I never liked New York before, but this night it was beautiful. I walked for blocks and blocks, I guess. Everything seemed different to me. It was raining softly and the city lights created a golden glow. Something had happened to me and I knew it."

"That's what you mean by accepting Christ—you just ask?" I was more puzzled than ever.

"That's it, as simple as that," Tom replied. "Of course, you have to want Jesus in your life, really want Him. That's the way it starts. And let me tell you, things then begin to change. Since then I have found a satisfaction and a joy about living that I simply never knew was possible."

The heat at that moment seemed unbearable as I wiped away drops of perspiration over my lip. The iced tea was soothing as I sipped it, although with Tom's points hitting home so painfully, I longed for a scotch and soda. To myself I admitted that Tom was on target: the world of us against them as we saw it from our insulated White House enclave—the Nixon White House against the world. Insecure about our cause, our overkill approach was a way to play it safe. And yet . . .

"Chuck, I don't think you understand what I'm saying about God until you are willing to face yourself honestly and squarely. This is the first step." Tom reached to the corner table and picked up a small paperback book. I read the title: *Mere Christianity* by C.S. Lewis.

"I suggest you take this with you and read it while you are on vacation." Tom started to hand it to me, then paused. "Let me read you one chapter."

I leaned back, still on the defensive, my mind and emotions whirling.

There is one vice . . . There is one fault . . . which we are more unconscious in ourselves. And the more we have it ourselves, the more we dislike it in others.

The vice I am talking of is Pride or Self-Conceit . . . Pride leads to every other vice: it is the complete anti-God state of mind.

As he read, I could feel a flush coming into my face and a curious burning sensation that made the night seem even warmer. Lewis's words seemed to pound straight at me.

. . . it is Pride which has been the chief cause of misery in every nation and every family since the world began. Other vices may sometimes bring people together: you may find good fellowship and jokes and friendliness among drunken people or unchaste people. But Pride always means enmity—it *is* enmity. And not only enmity between man and man, but enmity to God.

In God you come up against something which is in every respect immeasurably superior to yourself. Unless you know God as that—and, therefore, know yourself as nothing in comparison—you do not know God at all. As long as you are proud you cannot know God. A proud man is always looking down on things and people: and, of course, as long as you are looking down, you cannot see something that is above you.

Suddenly I felt naked and unclean, my bravado defenses gone. I was exposed, unprotected, for Lewis's words were describing me.

Now, sitting there on the dimly lit porch, my self-centered past was washing over me in waves. It was painful. Agony. Desperately I tried to defend myself. What about my sacrifices for government service, the giving up of a big income, putting my stocks into a blind trust? The truth, I saw in an instant, was that I'd wanted the position in the White House more than I'd wanted money. There was no sacrifice. And the more I had talked about my own sacrifices, the more I was really trying to build myself up in the eyes of others. I would eagerly have given up everything I'd ever earned to prove myself at the mountaintop of government. It was pride—Lewis's "great sin"—that had propelled me through life.

Tom finished the chapter on pride and shut the book. I mumbled something noncommittal to the effect that "I'll look forward to reading that." But Lewis's torpedo had hit me amidships. I think Phillips knew it as he stared into my eyes. That one chapter ripped through the protective armor in which I had unknowingly encased myself for forty-two years. Of course, I had not known God. How could I? I had been concerned with myself. I had done this and that, I had achieved, I had succeeded and I had given God none of the credit, never once thanking Him for any of His gifts to me. I had never thought of anything being "immeasurably superior" to myself, or if I had thought in fleeting moments about the infinite power of God, I had not related Him to my life. In those brief moments while Tom read, I saw myself as I never had before. And the picture was ugly.

"Tom, you've shaken me up. I'll admit that. That chapter describes me. But I can't tell you I'm ready to make the kind of commitment you did. I've got to be certain. I've got to learn a lot more, be sure all my reservations are satisfied. I've got a lot of intellectual hang-ups to get past."

For a moment Tom looked disappointed, then he smiled. "I understand, I understand."

But Tom did not press on. He handed me his copy of *Mere Christianity*. "Once you've read this, you might want to read the Book of John in the Bible." I scribbled notes of the key passages he quoted.

Tom walked me to the front door and bid me farewell.

Outside in the darkness, the iron grip I'd kept on my emotions began to relax. Tears welled up in my eyes as I groped in the darkness for the right key to start my car. Angrily I brushed them away and started the engine. "What kind of weakness is this?" I said to nobody.

The tears spilled over and suddenly I knew I had to go back into the house and pray with Tom. I turned off the motor, got out of the car. As I did, the kitchen light went out, then the light in the dining room. Through the hall window I saw Tom stand aside as Gert started up the stairs ahead of him. Now the hall was in darkness. It was too late. I stood for a moment staring at the darkened house, only one light burning now in an upstairs bedroom. Why hadn't I prayed when he gave me the chance? I wanted to so badly. Now I was alone, really alone.

As I drove out of Tom's driveway, the tears were flowing uncontrollably. There were no streetlights, no moonlight. The car headlights were flooding illumination before my eyes, but I was crying so hard it was like trying to swim underwater. I pulled to the side of the road not more than a hundred yards from the entrance to Tom's driveway, the tires sinking into soft mounds of pine needles.

I remember hoping that Tom and Gert wouldn't hear my sobbing, the only sound other than the chirping of crickets that penetrated the still of the night. With my face cupped in my hands, head leaning forward against the wheel, I forgot about machismo, about pretenses, about fears of being weak. And as I did, I began to experience a wonderful feeling of being released. Then came the strange sensation that water was not only running down my cheeks, but surging through my whole body as well, cleansing and cooling as it went. They weren't tears of sadness and remorse, nor of joy—but somehow, tears of relief.

And then I prayed my first real prayer. "God, I don't know how to find You, but I'm going to try! I'm not much the way I am now, but somehow I want to give myself to You." I didn't know how to say more, so I repeated over and over the words: Take me.

I stayed there in the car, wet-eyed, praying, thinking, for perhaps half an hour, perhaps longer, alone in the quiet of the dark night. Yet for the first time in my life I was not alone at all.

HUMILITY: THE PATH TO CHRIST

Chuck Colson recognized that his life was deeply flawed because of pride. Lewis's words were a wake-up call that spoke powerfully into his life, particularly the passage that said, "Pride is a spiritual cancer; it eats up the very possibility of love, or contentment . . ." All of his

PRIDE IS A SPIRITUAL CANCER; IT EATS UP THE VERY
POSSIBILITY OF LOVE, OR CONTENTMENT..." (C.S. LEWIS)

life he had been eaten up by pride and arrogance and he never knew it. He realized how it blinded him to spiritual truth.

During the next week while on vacation, Colson read *Mere Christianity* slowly and deliberately. As he wrestled with Lewis's words his eyes were opened. Finally, early one morning as he was all alone staring at the sea, he humbled his heart and prayed: "Lord Jesus, I believe You. I accept You. Please come into my life. I commit it to You."

Afterwards he said,

> With these few words that morning, while the briny sea churned, came a sureness of mind that matched the depth of feeling in my heart. There came something more: strength and serenity, a wonderful new assurance about life, a fresh perception of myself and the world around me. In the process, I felt old fears, tensions, and animosities draining away. I was coming alive to things I'd never seen before; as if God was filling the barren void I'd known for so many months, filling it to its brim with a whole new kind of awareness.

Charles Colson went on to spend seven months in a federal prison and then was released. He then founded "Prison Fellowship" that has ministered to millions of prisoners all over the world. He also became a distinguished author and speaker. Those who knew him best watched God completely transform his life. He died in 2012.

Colson's story is a picture of the theme of this book. Pride is deadly. Lewis says it has been the chief cause of misery in every nation and every family since the world began. On the other hand, humility is the eyes that allow us to see God. It unleashes His grace and strength into our lives and enables us to do that which we cannot do ourselves. Truly, there is power in the humble life.

AFTERWORDS

When I look at my life and my own spiritual journey, in many ways I was much like Chuck Colson. The great barrier that kept me from coming to faith was pride. Though I had always believed the Christian message to be true I chose to intentionally live without God in my life. The simple reason is that I loved the approval of man more than I loved the approval of God. I was like Pascal's friends who had no interest in spiritual truth because they feared the opinion of their friends and dreaded being labeled weak and religious. I too desired to court the favor of the worldly, popular and successful people in my sphere of influence. I had an image to keep up and an audience to impress.

Though life was good, something began to happen in me that was totally unexpected and which was completely out of my control. I began to experience an emptiness in my life that I could not understand. Over time I concluded that maybe I should start going to church hoping that the emptiness would disappear, but it didn't.

So I began what I would call a spiritual search, reading books and the Bible. I still believed the Christian message to be true, but I had hoped there was a way for me to be a Christian on my own terms. To be quite honest, I was afraid to become a Christian. I was afraid of how God would change my life and what people would think of me if I became a serious follower of Jesus. Yet the sense of an empty, meaningless life persisted.

Then through a series of circumstances, particularly when one of my closest friends was involved in a serious motorcycle accident, I came to a startling conclusion. A choice had to be made. I could not remain neutral towards Jesus. In fact, Christ Himself said, "You are either with Me or against Me." There is no middle ground.

I found myself in a situation similar to Jesus' disciples when Christ Himself confronted them with the necessity of a choice.

In the sixth chapter of John (vs. 66-69), many of his followers began to withdraw from Him and chose to no longer follow Him. They did not like what He was teaching. He is standing there, with only the twelve disciples remaining. He asks them "Do you not want to leave too and go with them?" Peter responds and says:

> Lord, to whom shall we go? You have words of eternal life. We have believed and have come to know that You are the Holy One of God.

What a powerful response by Peter. If we do not put our faith in You, Jesus, who will we look to for eternal life? Who will we put our hope and faith in? This is the question we are all confronted with. It is the choice we have to make. If I do not look to Christ for eternal life, to whom shall I look? Who will I rely upon?

As I recall, what caused me to wave the white flag and surrender was when I finally asked myself, "What is the alternative?" The alternative was to reject Christ's offer of the forgiveness of my sins, to reject His offer of eternal life, and to walk through life alone without Him. I could not reject Him. Therefore, one evening, I made the decision to humble myself, surrender to Christ, and put my faith in Him. All I can say is that since that day, my life has not been the same. Walking through life with Christ has been the ultimate adventure, and I never dreamed that my life with Him as my guide would have turned out so well.

ACKNOWLEDGEMENTS
AND SOURCES

I am first and foremost grateful to all of my family, friends, and colleagues here at The Center for Executive Leadership who have encouraged me along the way as I worked on this project. Most significantly, I want to thank Kim Knott who has worked tirelessly to see this book become a reality.

I would be remiss if I did not acknowledge several individuals whose work greatly influenced and shape the substance of this book. Primarily C.S. Lewis, Tim Keller and Pat Williams, whose work has profoundly shaped my thinking and perspective on the issue of "humility."

Finally, as with any writing, I acknowledge that I am standing on the shoulders of those who have come before me, with deep appreciation to the many people whose writing have informed this work.

SOURCES

Arevanye, "A C.S. Lewis Blog" from "The Window in the Garden Wall", North Atlanta, GA, 2005.

Becker, Ernest, *The Denial of Death*, Free Press, New York, NY, 1973.

Boorstin, Daniel J., *The Image: A Guide to Pseudo-Events in America*, Vintage Books, New York, NY, 1992.

Bosch, Henry, *Encyclopedia of 7,700 Illustrations*, Assurance Publishers, Rockville, MD, 1985.

Brand, Paul, Yancey, Philip, *Pain: The Gift Nobody Wants*, Harper Collins Publishers, Zondervan, Grand Rapids, MI, 1993.

Brooks, David, *The Road to Character*, Random House, New York, NY, 1993.

Brubach, Holly, "Enough About You," *The New York Times*, 2009.

Collins, Jim, *How the Mighty Fall*, Harper Collins, New York, NY, 2009.

Colson, Charles, *Born Again*, Chosen Books, Lincoln, VA, 1976

Coutu, Diane "I Was Greedy Too," *Harvard Business Review*, Aug, 2003.

Dickson, John, *Humillitas*, Zondervan, Grand Rapids, MI, 2011.

Douglas, Lloyd C., *Magnificent Obsession*, Grossell and Dunlap, New York, NY, 1929.

Durant, Will, *The Story of Civilization: Caesar and Christ—A History of Roman Civilization and Christianity from Their Beginnings to A. C. 325 Through 557*, Simon & Schuster, Inc. New York, NY, 1935–1975.

Freitas, Donna, *The Happiness Effect*, Oxford University Press, New York, NY, 2017

Friedman, Thomas L., "How to Get a Job at Google," *The New York Times*, 2-22-3024.

George, David, Akin, Daniel L., Holman *Old Testament Commentary, Ecclesiastes, Song of Songs, Holman Reference*, Broad Man and Holman, Nashville, TN, 2003.

Guinness, Os, *Steering Through Chaos, When No One Sees*, NAVPRESS, Colorado Springs, CO 2000.

Guinness, Os, *The Call*, Word Publishing, Nashville, TN, 1998.

Holiday, Ryan, *Ego Is the Enemy*, Penquin Random House, New York, New York, 2016.

Jenkins, Rob, "Dr. King and the Power of Humility", Gwinnett Daily Post, Atlanta, GA, 01-12-2017

Jones, Thomas, *The Prideful Soul's Guide to Humility*, Good Book Press, Springhill, TN. 1973.

Keller, Timothy, *Counterfeit Gods*, Penquin Group-Dutton, New York, NY, 2009.

Keller, Timothy, "Pride; The Case of Nebuchadnezzar—The Seven Deadly Sins," Sermon, Redeemer Presbyterian Church, New York, NY, 02-05-1995.

Keller, Timothy, "Humility—The Real Signs of the Spirit," Sermon, Redeemer Presbyterian Church, New York, NY, 05-23-2010.

Knappenberger, Brian, "Larry Ellison," TV Segment, "Bloomberg Game Changer, New York, NY, 12-02-2010.

Leung, Rebecca, "Hidden Truth: Lori Hacking Case," News Segment, CBS News, 08-05-2004.

Marsh, Jason, Keltner, Dacher, "Thanksgiving and Gratitude: The Science of Happier Holidays," *Wall Street Journal*, 11-28-2014.

Murray, Andrew, *Humility*, Christian Literature Crusade, Fort Washington, PA, 1980.

Nicholson, Jeremy, "How Gratitude Influences Loving Behavior," *Psychology Today*, 09-28-2011.

Nouwen, Henri, *The Return of the Prodigal Son*, Deckle Edge, Image, Memphis, TN, 1994.

Prince, Derek, *Pride Versus Humility*, Whitaker House, New Kensington PA, 2016.

Root, Andrew, "Never Let Them See You Cry," *Christianity Today*, Carol Stream, IL, 2017.

Rosin, Hanna, "The Silicon Valley Suicides," *The Atlantic*" Boston, MA, 2015.

Simmons III, Richard E., *Reliable Truth*, Union Hill Publishing, Birmingham, AL 2013.

Simmons III, Richard E., *The True Measure of a Man*, Union Hill Publishing, Birmingham, AL 2011.

Smith, Adam, *The Theory of Moral Sentiments*, 1759.

Stott, John, *Your Mind Matters: The Place of the Mind in the Christian Life*, InterVarsity Press, Downers Grove, IL, 1972.

Twenge, Jean, Campbell, W. Keith, *The Narcissism Epidemic*, Simon & Schuster, Inc., New York, NY, 2009.

Vanity Fair, April 1991, Vol. 54, Iss.4, pg. 160-169, 196-202, by: Lynn Hirschberg, "The Misfit"

Veblen, Thorstein, *The Theory of the Leisure Class*, Macmillan, New York, NY, 1899.

Vitz, Paul, Dr., edited by Dallas Willard, *A Place for Truth*, IVP Books, Downers Grove, IL, 2010.

Walker, Sam, "The Seven Secrets of Great Team Captains," *Wall Street Journal*, New York, New York, 2017.

Wikipedia, "Osama bin Laden" St. Petersburg, FL. 2017.

Wikipedia, "Charles Colson" St. Petersburg, FL. 2017.

Willard, Dallas, *A Place for Truth*, InterVarsity Press, Downers Grove, FL 2010.

Willard, Dallas, *The Spirit of the Disciplines*, Harcourt Brace, New York, NY, 1991.

Williams, Pat, *Humility*, Shiloh Run Press, Uhrichsville, OH, 2016.

Yancey, Philip, *The Jesus I Never Knew* as cited in Durant, Wills, *The Story of Civilization*, Simon & Schuster, Inc., New York, NY, 1935–1975.

Yancey, Philip, *What Good is God, Faith Words*, Zondervan, Grand Rapids, MI, 2010.

Zacharias, Ravi, *Jesus Among Other Gods*, Word Publishing, Nashville, TN, 2000.

ALSO BY RICHARD E. SIMMONS III

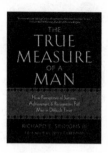

THE TRUE MEASURE OF A MAN

How Perceptions of Success, Achievement & Recognition Fail Men in Difficult Times

In our performance-driven culture this book provides liberating truth on how to be set free from the fear of failure, comparing ourselves to others and the false ideas we have about masculinity.

THE REASON FOR LIFE

Why Did God Put Me Here?

This book seeks to help people answer the question "What is the reason for life?' by first posing a second pivotal question, which is: "Why did God put me here?"

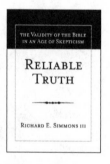

A LIFE OF EXCELLENCE

Wisdom for Effective Living

A Life of Excellence lays out three principles that clearly point to a life of excellence. I am convinced that if one lives in accordance with these principles, their life will flourish and prosper.

RELIABLE TRUTH

The Validity of the Bible in an Age of Skepticism

Do you believe the Bible is the inspired word of God? Reliable Truth offers powerful and compelling evidence why the Bible is valid and true.

ALSO BY RICHARD E. SIMMONS III

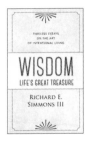

WISDOM: LIFE'S GREAT TREASURE

Timeless Essays on the Art of Intentional Living

A collection of short essays on wisdom to serve as a guide to help people walk in wisdom on their journey towards a healthy and meaningful life.

SAFE PASSAGE

Thinking Clearly about Life & Death

Safe Passage examines C. S. Lewis's thoughts and perspective on the issue of human mortalit.

AUTHOR CONTACT

Richard E. Simmons III welcomes inquiries and is available for speaking opportunities to groups, meetings and conferences.

- Email Richard at richard@thecenterbham.org
- Visit our website at www.richardesimmons3.com

 @thecenterbham   @thecenterbham

 @thecentertweets   Richard E Simmons III